MARK GORMAN

GOD'S PLAN

for

PROSPERITY

A BALANCED PERSPECTIVE ON

FINANCIAL WEALTH

First Printing, September 2004
Second Printing, February 2005

ISBN 0-9761428-0-5

Book design: Dreambox Creative. 916.705.0406. www.dreamboxcreative.com

Dedication

⌒

This book is dedicated to my wonderful wife,
Gina and our children, Kenneth & Sharah, who loved and
supported me during the writing of this book.

Other than my relationship with Jesus Christ, they are the
most important people in my life.

ENDORSEMENTS FOR
"God's Plan For Prosperity"

Dr. C. Peter Wagner:

I wish that every believer today would listen to Mark Gorman. Nothing can shackle the spread of the gospel more than the insidious spirit of poverty that binds so many of God's people. But God's Plan for Prosperity is the answer! It will bring immediate deliverance to every reader who is willing to follow these clear biblical principles. I love this book!

C. PETER WAGNER, PRESIDING APOSTLE
INTERNATIONAL COALITION OF APOSTLES

Dr. John Kelly:

The first thought that came to my mind after I read this excellent book was - where was it when I was pasturing! Why? Because I would have made an investment in the future financial harvest of my church by purchasing this book and giving it to all the members!

God's Plan for Prosperity is more than a balanced perspective on financial wealth and we need that. It is a book full of knowledge, principles and revelation. Mark Gorman educates and imparts to the reader present day prophetic truth and this truth will set you free! This book is a key to unlock the doors to your financial prosperity.

APOSTLE JOHN P. KELLY
PRESIDENT, LEAD (LEADERSHIP EDUCATION FOR APOSTOLIC DEVELOPMENT)

Dr. Mike Murdock:

"When Mark Gorman speaks, I listen. Few of his caliber are left today. He is relentlessly scriptural, precise and accurate and unfailingly compassionate in helping people obtain their dreams and goals. He has been a personal and consistent true friend of my lifetime. Every serious seeker of an uncommon and productive life should make this book MUST reading. "

DR. MIKE MURDOCK
THE WISDOM CENTER

John DiLemme:

I label this book a *Five-Star* winner and you owe it to yourself to read it..TODAY! Don't miss out on your Harvest! I've read over 1,000+ books in my life, and Chapter 10 in this book is all you need to manifest the blessings that are stored up for you! Mark's straightforward, uncomplicated, revealing yet truthfully challenging wisdom is one-of-a-kind! The book is a *MUST OWN* for your personal success library. I owe a huge thanks to Mark Gorman for caring enough to lay out the biblical financial strategies that will result in people living their God-Given Dream!

JOHN DI LEMME
INTERNATIONAL MOTIVATIONAL SPEAKER - BUSINESS SUCCESS COACH

http://www.FindYourWhy.com

CONTENTS

CHAPTER 1

∽ℯ⌒

HOW MUCH MONEY SHOULD A CHRISTIAN HAVE?

"How much money is too much for a Christian to have?"

It was 1994, and I was in Auckland, New Zealand. Having just come off stage from speaking at a business convention, I was approached by a young couple who explained that they were not actually in business with the rest of the people at this event. Instead, they had come as spectators – guests of some of the business owners attending the convention. Their primary reason for attending was that they had heard that I, a minister, would be speaking there, and they wanted to hear my "take" on business – specifically wealth. They explained that, as Christians, they were very uncomfortable in this setting, because of the emphasis on money.

Then, they looked at me and asked, "How much money is too much for a Christian to have?"

I replied, "You can't have too much money."

Their shock was evident. They were not expecting this answer from a preacher.

In response, I told them something which I believe to be a foundational principle regarding wealth, "It is not what I have that makes me evil. It's what I love that makes me evil."

The Bible does not say that having money is evil. Instead, it says that loving money is evil. **"For the love of money is the root of all evil…"** 1 Timothy 6:5 (KJV)

For years, many Christians have assumed that the only people who love money are the ones who have it. But my contention is that most of the people who love money, don't have any. Why? Because God can't trust them with it. They love it too much.

Conversely, there are many people who have money, but don't love it. They have proven to God that they love Him more than they love money. For that reason, He not only trusts them with money, but He makes sure that they have plenty.

Why? Because 2 Corinthians 9:11 (NIV) says, **"You will be made rich in every way so that you can be generous on every occasion ..."**

God is looking for generous people, so He can put wealth in their hands, enabling them to "make a difference" in this world. If a greedy person has wealth, they only enhance their own life. But a generous person, with financial abundance, can provide substantial support to the work of God, while also helping to make significant changes in the lives of others.

I grew up in church. My dad was a pastor. In that environment, I often heard of the evils of wealth. Many people taught us that financial prosperity was evil. And might I add, we did an excellent job of avoiding it. We were nowhere near prosperity.

Seriously, for many years I believed that a Christian's income should be restricted to a modest amount, which provided for their needs and little more. I still believe that if a person loves money, they should have only enough to live on.

"IT IS NOT WHAT I HAVE THAT MAKES ME EVIL. IT'S WHAT I LOVE THAT MAKES ME EVIL."

In Matthew chapter 19, and Mark chapter 10, we find the story of the rich young ruler. This young man came to Jesus, telling Him of all the things he had done to please God. He then asked, "What else should I do?" Jesus told him to sell all he had, and give it to the poor.

Upon hearing this, the young man became sorrowful, realizing that he did not love God as much as he had thought. In reality, he actually loved money more than he loved God. He lowered his head and walked away, leaving the Master.

Jesus then turned to His disciples, who had observed this incident. He explained that it is easier for a camel to go through the eye of a needle, than for a rich person to enter the Kingdom of God.

On one of my visits to the Holy Land, while in the city of Jerusalem, I saw "the eye of a needle". This is a small, narrow doorway which leads into the temple area. In order for a camel to go through this doorway, two requirements must be met: first, all material provisions which the camel is carrying must be removed from its body. Second, the camel must crawl on its knees in order to get low enough to pass through this short opening.

Jesus knew that this young man loved money. He had come to Jesus, practically boasting of his devotion and allegiance to God, implying that God really was first in his life. In order to help him see that this was not the case, Jesus identified the one thing in his life which he loved more than God.

You see, anything which we love more than God, becomes sin, regardless of what or who it may be. In two different chapters of the book of Matthew, chapters 5 and 18, Jesus tells us that if our eye causes us to sin, we should pluck it out. Did He literally mean that we should remove our eyes from their sockets in order to live a Godly life? Absolutely not. Jesus was simply trying to help us understand that we shouldn't let anything come between us and God, regardless of how important it may be to us.

In the case of the rich young ruler, Jesus knew that he would be better off without anything which meant more to him than God. Some people have taken this story literally, to mean that we should be penniless; giving everything we have to the poor. I do not believe that, anymore than I would believe that in order to be Christians, we must pluck out our eyes.

When Jesus went on to speak of how difficult it is for a rich person to come to God, He implied that they should be willing to leave their material possessions, and humble themselves, just as the camel must get on its knees to go through that doorway.

When a person has great wealth, and does not know Christ, they have a tendency to become dependent on that wealth for their fulfillment. Often, their self image is found in their financial standing and the lifestyle their wealth provides. In order for them to accept Christ, like the rest of us, they must make Him first in their life – even before their possessions. This is why they must be prepared to emulate the camel, establishing the fact that God is more important than their money, and that they are willing to humble themselves before Him.

Again, many Christians have misinterpreted the meaning of this statement by Jesus, assuming that it is impossible to be a Christian, and have wealth at the same time.

First of all, Jesus did not say that it is impossible for a rich person to be saved. He only said that it is difficult. Because I speak in the business community as well as the church, I have had the opportunity to lead many wealthy people to Christ, so I know, from personal experience, that a rich person can enter the Kingdom of God.

Secondly, I am convinced that this entire story teaches us that it is easier for a Christian to become a millionaire, than for a millionaire to become a Christian.

If you have accepted Christ, and He is first in your life, and you have a generous heart, I believe He wants you to be rich. That's what 2 Corinthians 9:11 tells us. Why would He tell us that we will be made rich, if it is impossible to be a rich Christian?

It costs money to spread the Gospel. God is looking for generous people, through whom He can funnel provision into His kingdom work here on earth. Unfortunately, however, there are many generous Christians who think wealth is evil, and they are running from it. Therefore, even though they are generous, they can't make much of a difference, because of their limited financial resources.

Often, the same people who tell you that we shouldn't have much money, will turn around and tell you to be a Good Samaritan. Do you remember that story? Jesus told the parable of a man who came to the aid of someone who had been beaten and robbed, and left for dead.

Do you realize that most Christians could not afford to be a Good Samaritan without using a credit card? Imagine finding someone on the side of the road – their car has been stolen, their money is gone, and they are badly wounded, in need of medical attention. Could you afford to take care of all of their medical needs – take them to a hotel – pay for their room for a week in advance – pay for their breakfast for a week – lunch for a week – dinner for a week – and say to the hotel clerk that you will be back at the end of the week to pay any other expenses they incurred? Can you imagine doing all of this with cash? Remember, in the Bible days, they did not have credit cards. In reality, most Christians could not afford to do this, yet we are told by many to avoid wealth.

Broke people can't help broke people. You and I need to be in a position which affords us the ability to make a difference in someone else's life.

On several occasions people have told me proudly, "I am not greedy. All I want is enough to pay my bills." My reply is, "Well, you may not be greedy, but you sure are selfish. You should want more than enough to pay your bills. You should want enough to have extra, so you can help someone else."

> "BROKE PEOPLE CAN'T HELP BROKE PEOPLE."

Recently, I sat at lunch with a minister friend who was warning me of the evils of prosperity. And I can tell you, if prosperity really is evil…

he is nowhere near it. In fact, I was paying for lunch.

I asked him, "Don't you want to help people?" His face lit up with a smile. "Yes," he said, "I love helping people." I informed him that the previous week, my wife and I had handed a $10,000 check to a missionary. I said, "Do you know what a missionary's face looks like when they receive a $10,000 check?" "No," he replied.

"And you never will" I said, "Because you have no intention of ever having enough money to do that."

I looked at my friend and said, "We gave that $10,000 to help build a church in Mexico. Do you think it would have been better if we had been broke, and wrote them a note?"

Like so many other Christians, he is running from prosperity because he believes it is evil. His generosity will benefit very few people because he has so little with which to be generous.

A generous Christian with a lot of money can really hurt the work of the devil, and help the work of God.

I was given the tape pack, "God's Plan For Prosperity". After hearing it, I was convicted about my giving habits [I didn't have any.] I am unemployed, my last check from my previous job came in Friday. I determined that if I was going to test it, I had to give at least 20% to "good ground". In the span of 5 days, I had a call back on a job that was offered to someone else who changed their mind, got a call on a second, spoke to a buddy about a third job, received my tax return a week earlier than expected, and God directed us to the mini-van deal of a lifetime. Thank you for being forthright, honest, and tough. We continue to tithe and sow seeds, and we are excited to see what's next.
[SENT TO OUR OFFICE VIA EMAIL]

Thank you so much for allowing us to plant a seed in your ministry. We came to rededicate our lives to the Lord at a business conference. We have been in business for 2 years but have never been able to get things going for us. Since we planted our "seed of harvest" and you have been praying for us, we have had two new business clients and the third one is coming soon.
[D. H. OF WEST VIRGINIA]

I attended a Texas leadership conference. You ministered that Sunday morning and fortunately I took my 15-year-old daughter. Please know that your message that morning touched both my daughter and me. She is a delightful kid but being a single parent is challenging nonetheless. I sowed $150.00 that morning knowing that I really couldn't afford to do so but your message was so powerful, I had faith that all would work out well and it did. The following day I received my annual review at work and got a bonus besides.
[B. S. OF TEXAS]

CHAPTER 2

∞⊛

WEALTH

At this point, you may be saying to yourself, "I agree with everything Mark is saying about wealth, because it seems that God's only purpose in prospering us is so we will give it away."

Stop and think about it. 2 Corinthians 9:11 says that we will be made rich in every way so we can be generous. It does not say we will be made rich so we can become poor, after giving it all away. If you give everything away, you will cease to be rich, and will no longer have the means to be generous.

In the previous verse, 2 Corinthians 9:10, Paul states that God gives the sower two things: seed to sow and bread for food. Every time God gives you something, it will consist of both of these: seed to sow and bread for food. You shouldn't eat it all, and you shouldn't sow it all. Eat the bread and sow the seed.

If you plant an entire peach, would its harvest produce any more fruit than if you would have only planted the seed? No, there is no benefit derived by planting the fruit with the seed. Therefore, if you plant an entire peach, you are being wasteful – a poor steward with what God has placed in your hand.

God has prospered me. I live a comfortable life. I have never tried to hide that fact.

Sometimes, people will approach me and ask, "Mark, since God has blessed you financially, why don't you give it all away?"

I say, "If that is the way you feel, then I assume that is what you are doing too, which would mean that you are now homeless. Which cardboard box did you sleep in last night?" (I know that sounds sarcastic on my part, but I find it amazing that a complete stranger would feel comfortable in rebuking me about my finances, and telling me how to manage my money.)

When I say this, they typically reply, "Oh, I didn't mean that you should give it ALL away. I only meant that you should give most of it away."

This seems to be an ongoing dilemma for every Christian; how much should I spend on myself and how much should I give?

If you want to know how much to give away and how much to keep, eat a peach, and you'll figure it out. I have never seen anyone eat an entire peach. They always leave something behind.

There comes a certain point in eating a peach when you lose the desire to take another bite. This is because you have run out of "bread for food" and now, all you have left is "seed to sow".

God created the seed with two specific qualities:

1. When you eat what you should have planted, it will leave a bad taste in your mouth.

2. When you eat the seed, it will cause great pain.

If your finances are leaving a bad taste in your mouth, and causing pain, it is very likely that you are eating what you should have planted.

"GOD'S INTENTION HAS ALWAYS BEEN FOR US TO BE BLESSED WITH INCREASE, WHEN WE LIVE BY, AND RESPECT THE LAWS, WHICH HE HAS ESTABLISHED."

When you plant a peach seed, it will produce a tree, which will then yield fruit. Many peaches will result from the one seed. This harvest not only gives you a generous supply of seeds to sow, but it also produces an abundant return of "bread for food".

God has created a "reward system", which blesses the person who has a generous heart. He does not intend for us to feel obligated to give away the bounty with which He has rewarded our generosity. Nor does He want us to feel guilty for enjoying the benefits of our harvest.

Imagine the outcome of planting all of those peach seeds from your first harvest. This would result in many, many more trees, which would produce hundreds, and even thousands of peaches, giving you even more seed to sow, and more fruit for you to enjoy.

If you understand farming, it's not hard to see that God's intention has always been for us to be blessed with increase, when we live by, and respect the laws which He has established.

Genesis 8:22(NIV) says, **"As long as the earth endures, seedtime and harvest...will never cease"**. This is one of God's laws. When we cooperate with His laws, they work to our advantage, and in result, we are blessed.

Many people believe that the blessings of God are only manifested as spiritual experiences and emotional well being. My contention is that if a farmer plants corn, he will receive corn in return. When you plant finances, God will bless you financially. We need to get "comfortable" with the concept of wealth.

Proverbs 13:22 states that a good man leaves an inheritance to his children's children. Obviously, this is telling us that God intends for us to be in a financial position which would enable us to leave significant finances to our heirs.

—— ❧ ——

"AS YOU READ THE BIBLE, YOU FIND THAT GOD'S PEOPLE WERE VERY OFTEN, THE WEALTHIEST PEOPLE OF THEIR DAY. "

When I shared this with someone, to explain God's position on prosperity, their reply was that this verse is speaking of an inheritance of Godliness, character and integrity.

I said, "No, I think it means cash."

Look at the second half of this verse. In fact, let's look at the entire verse, so you will see what God is saying:

"A good man leaves an inheritance to his children's children, But the wealth of the sinner

is stored up for the righteous". Proverbs 13:22 (NKJV)

I then said, "Do you think that the wealth of the sinner is a wealth of Godliness, character, and integrity? No, it's cash."

It seems obvious to me that our ability to leave a generous inheritance is part of the "bread for food" in 2 Corinthians 9:10.

As I stated previously, God has prospered me and blessed our family with a nice lifestyle. A while back, someone told me, "Mark, for a preacher, I think you are too materialistic."

I said, "Well, if you think I'm materialistic, you are going to hate Heaven... streets of gold... walls of jasper... gates of pearl and everyone living in mansions."

If God was as opposed to wealth as some people think, all the buildings in Heaven would be made of cinder blocks with tin roofs, and the streets would be dirt roads. When you think about it, if God was opposed to prosperity, He certainly would not have designed Heaven in the way He did.

Why did God use a place of such extravagant wealth to motivate us to live a Godly life? He could have simply described beautiful meadows filled with wildflowers, sunny skies and cool breezes, with worship music playing softly in the background. Instead, He described tangible symbols of financial prosperity as the ingredients for the ultimate destination for a child of God.

The notion that we are glorifying God by living below the poverty level, or barely existing on what we make, is completely illogical. My children's lifestyle is a direct reflection of my ability to provide, and my generosity toward my family. The same is true of our Heavenly Father.

As you read the Bible, you find that God's people were very often, the wealthiest people of their day.

Abraham was one of the wealthiest men of his day. His nephew, Lot, benefited from his association with Abraham, which resulted in his own prosperity.

Job was one of the wealthiest men of his day, and after his season of testing, in which he proved to be faithful to God, he was blessed with double, and became even wealthier. In fact, as you read the book of Job, you can see that Job's wealth is actually described as a testimony to God's blessing on his life.

David was described as a man after God's own heart, and he became extremely wealthy. His son, Solomon, the wisest man who ever lived, was even more prosperous. The Queen of Sheba heard of Solomon's wisdom, and came to visit him. After he answered all her questions, she was amazed not only with his wisdom but also, his tremendous wealth.

When the children of Israel left Egypt's bondage, the Egyptians gave them their silver and gold. God arranged for them to receive financial abundance as a symbol of His provision in their lives.

I have never encountered a Christian who had any qualms about saying that "God owns the cattle of a thousand hills." It seems that they have no problem with the thought of God being wealthy, but they can't see themselves being prosperous. And again, I will say that, if they love money and do not have a generous heart, they should not be rich!

One of the most well known verses of scripture in the Bible is John 3:16. It states that God so loved the world that He gave His only Son. God is a giver. If we are going to be like Him, we must be givers too.

If your life emulates God, with a generous, giving heart, God wants to reward you by bringing greater abundance into your life.

Matthew 25:21 states that if we are faithful over a "few things", we will be made ruler over "many things". One of the things this applies to is money. God gives seed to the sower. When we prove that we have the heart to sow, He makes sure we don't run out of seed. God wants you to prosper.

I am writing you to tell you what happened to my husband and I since we gave our seed of faith of $100. My husband got a call to build a house, and netted a profit of $14,000! Not only did our family benefit from this job, but 3 other families who were in need received miracles as well. Thank you again for your support and tapes.
[L. B. FROM MICHIGAN]

We wanted to plant a seed at a leadership conference held in your honor. We were so blessed and our lives have not been the same since. That evening, in between services, we came home and organized all of our bills and talked about plans to make sure that things do not go awry again. You see, we've been suffering badly the past four months. We were unorganized and being poor stewards by not keeping a tight reign on our finances. We both tried to keep up with things but trying just wasn't enough. Your message was so timely. We were hurting badly and the message truly has delivered us. In all of the teachings that we've ever had on finances, this one was the one that made sense. In fact, it was almost scary the amount of sense it made.
[B. Y. OF GEORGIA]

We had not expected to receive a seed so soon after your visit to our church, but we got it exactly 7 weeks later. My dad had sent us a package for Christmas with a message to not open it until Christmas day. Well, on Christmas morning, I tore into the box only to find a large envelope. I opened that to find a smaller envelope. This continued until, 5 envelopes later, I opened a card with Jesus on the front that played "We Wish You a Merry Christmas" in a little electronic tune. In the card was a check for $1,000.00. Isn't Jesus great? I got a miracle for Christmas!
[W. T. OF GEORGIA]

CHAPTER 3

THE REWARDS OF GENEROSITY

A bare light bulb dangled in mid-air – the only source of light in that little church. The people sat on make-shift benches, constructed from discarded pieces of wood, which had been found in that small Mexican village. There were no windows in the building, only holes in the walls through which the air could circulate from outside. I stood, sharing the Word of God with these precious people, as the interpreter helped them to understand the message God had stirred in my heart.

During the message, I felt led to share with the people about sowing and reaping. As I taught Biblical financial principles, I heard someone just outside the building stumbling around in the dark, among the chickens and dogs in the village. At the end of my message, I noticed a man entering the doorway of the church wearing only a pair of red gym shorts. His dark, leathery skin had been weathered with time, and was now covered with dirt, from his tousled hair to his bare feet. It was obvious that he had not bathed in quite some time. Drunk on Tequila, he staggered into the church, yelling out something in Spanish, and carrying a cardboard box. He made his way down the aisle, walking directly toward me with the box in front of him. The interpreter told me that he was saying, "This is my offering for God. I want to be free."

When the box was laid at our feet, and the lid was removed, we found it filled with plums, which had been picked from one of the trees in the village. This little man had obviously heard my teaching as he stumbled around outside the church that night. He understood what I taught, that every harvest begins with a seed. With the help of the interpreter, we led him to Christ. After he repeated the prayer, asking God to forgive his sin, and inviting Jesus into his heart, I laid my hand on his head and asked God to free him from alcoholism. Instantly, he was sobered. He had already received the harvest he requested.

One of my favorite sayings by Thomas Edison is, "Most people don't recognize opportunity because it is usually dressed in overalls and looks like work."

Too often, when people ask God to give them a seed to sow, they assume that they should wait by the door, until the seed has been delivered to their house. This precious little Mexican man did not wait for God to put seed in his hand. Instead, he recognized an opportunity which God had placed before him – a tree filled with plums.

You become a sower in your heart before you ever sow with your hand. When God sees that your heart's desire is to sow, He identifies you as a sower and starts the process of getting the seed into your hand.

My number one goal, in regard to finances, is to give at least a million dollars to missions every year. That is why I know that God will continue to prosper me more and more. 2 Corinthians 9:10 says that God gives seed to the sower. If it is in your heart to sow, He will provide a way for you to get the seed. Now it may involve work on your part, you may even have to climb a tree to pick a few plums, but He will help you get the seed.

Some of my preacher friends have told me that I should not teach sowing and reaping in poor countries, because the people there do not understand it. Funny, I thought that's why we teach - because people don't understand a principle.

"EVERY HARVEST BEGINS WITH A SEED."

The first time I ever ministered in Africa, it was in the country of Ivory Coast, or as they say in French, Cote d'Ivoire. As I was flying from the United States to Cote d'Ivoire, the Lord spoke to me, and instructed me to teach on three main topics while there: Spiritual Warfare, Mentoring, and Sowing & Reaping.

At the end of one of the services, a tall, slender African lady walked up to me, accompanied by one of the interpreters. In her outstretched hand, she offered me an envelope which had one word written on it: sacrifice. Apparently, this word is spelled the same in French and English.

As I took the envelope in my hand, it felt thick. The interpreter said, "God told her to give you this offering."

"No!" I said, "God has blessed me. I didn't come to Africa to receive an offering. I came here at my own expense, to be a blessing to these people. I don't want their money."

The interpreter looked at me and said, "If you don't take this, you will offend her."

Suddenly, I heard a voice I've heard before. I heard it not with my ears, but in my spirit. It was the voice of the Holy Spirit.

He said, "She's one of your 300. You need to get her name, because you will be praying for her for the next year."

(For the past several years, I have asked God, each year, to give me 300 people who would sow a $1,000 seed into our ministry. I have made a covenant agreement with God that for one year, I will pray for them every day for three harvests: household salvation, healing & health, and abundance in finances. I keep a list of their names with me at all times.)

As I stood, looking at this precious, African lady, in my heart, I was having an argument with God. I was thinking, "God, you know I am blessed. I certainly don't need a poor person from Africa to be one of 'The 300'."

Again, God spoke to my spirit and instructed me to take the envelope, saying, "If you give this back to her, you will be handing her an envelope filled with seed. And she doesn't need seed – she needs harvest." I took her hand in mine, and asked her name. The interpreter informed me that her name was Constance. As the interpreter translated my words into French, I prayed a prayer with Constance, making a covenant with her and with God that I would faithfully pray for her every day for the next year.

When I returned to my hotel room, I opened the envelope to find 150,000 Francs. That sounds like a lot of money, doesn't it? It was actually worth about $180 USD. I said, "Lord, I don't care what its worth in US Dollars, I know that this was a lot more to her than $1,000. So as far as I'm concerned she's one of 'The 300'."

That day, I added Constance to the list of people I was praying for on a daily basis. Two weeks later, I was preaching in Buffalo, NY for Pastor Tommy Reid. My wife, Gina, was with me on that trip. Just before we left the hotel for the Sunday morning service, I told Gina that I felt I should check email one more time.

When I went online, there was a message from Fred Davis, the missionary in Africa, in Cote d'Ivoire. He said that Constance had asked him to let me know that when she handed me that envelope filled with money, it was the most difficult thing she had ever done. At that time, her finances were the worst they had ever been. But, after she placed the envelope in my hand, the very next week, her finances turned around. She had experienced a breakthrough, and her financial situation was now better than ever.

You see, God's laws work in any country. Sowing and reaping is not limited to the USA. It works all over the world.

A few weeks later, after receiving Fred's email, I was in Illinois, ministering on a telethon for a Christian television network. That night, I shared Constance's testimony with the television audience. Later that evening, I took a break for a few minutes while someone was singing. While walking down the hall of the television station, I was approached by a big man with broad shoulders. His name was Frank. There were tears in his eyes as he spoke to me.

He said, "Mark, I am supposed to be one of your '300'."

I said, "Oh, no! I'm not here to receive an offering for my ministry. I'm here raising money for this television network."

He replied, "Oh, don't worry about them. I've already given generously to them. But I know that God told me to support your ministry." He looked into my eyes and said, "I'm not going to give you $1,000. I'm going to give you $1,820 to make up the difference for Constance. Now, she has given $1,000 too."

I took him by the hand and we prayed, as I made a covenant with him and with God that I would pray for him and his family every day for the next year, believing God for abundant harvest in their lives.

Whether you are in Mexico, Africa or America, God's laws work all the time, and He wants you to prosper.

I wanted to share some wonderful news with you. My wife and I came forward the Sunday night you were here to tell you that the Lord had impressed both of us, at the same time, to be one of your 300 for 2004. About a month later, my wife had her annual review at work. Not only did she get a promotion, she received a 20% raise which amounted to about 6 times the amount we pledged to your ministry for 2004 (makes us wonder if we should have pledged more). God is faithful.
[B. C. FROM MISSOURI]

My breakthrough began over 3 years ago. The Holy Spirit confirmed in my heart that I needed to sow a $1000 seed. In spite of my circumstances, I wrote the check that night and watched as miracle after miracle began happening in my life. I sowed another $1000 into my church a year later and the third $1000 into Mark Ministries, Inc. Within 30 days after the third seed, I had a prospect for the building and within 90 days, I sold the building for $300,000. A one hundred-fold return! I am still rejoicing and I know there's more to come.
[D. S. FROM TENNESSEE]

While attending a fall leadership, we pledged to your ministry. It was truly a step out in faith because we did not have the money. Just this past week, we received a check for $1,300.00. We just wanted you to know so you could rejoice with us.
[J. A. OF TEXAS]

CHAPTER 4

∽૭୵

THE FOUR TYPES OF GIVING
⁻ TITHE ⁻

There are four types of giving taught in the Bible. The first of these is tithing. Leviticus 27:30 (NKJV) says, "**And all the tithe of the land, whether of the seed of the land or of the fruit of the tree, is the Lord's. It is holy to the Lord**". This same passage in the New Living Translation states, "**A tenth of the produce of the land, whether grain or fruit, belongs to the Lord and must be set apart to Him as holy**".

The word tithe means "tenth". God's word teaches us that the first ten percent of everything that comes into our hands, is already God's property, even before we receive it. Every time your boss pays you, he gives you your money and God's money. (He's already taken out the government's portion!)

Tithing is not a suggestion or an option. It is commanded by God. Malachi 3:8-12 (NKJV) says, "**Will a man rob God? Yet you have robbed Me! But you say, 'In what way have we robbed You?' In tithes and offerings. You are cursed with a curse, For you have robbed Me, Even this whole nation. Bring all the tithes into the storehouse, That there may be food in My house, And try Me now in this,**" Says the LORD of hosts, "**If I will not open for you the windows of heaven And pour out for you such blessing, That there will not be room enough to receive it. And I will rebuke the devourer for your sakes, So that he will not destroy the fruit of your ground, Nor shall the vine fail to bear fruit for you in the field,**" Says the LORD of hosts; "**And all nations will call you blessed, For you will be a delightful land,**" Says the LORD of hosts.

Isn't it great, that God offers to reward us for giving His property to Him? He could just say, "Give me my money or I'll send somebody over to your house!" Instead, He blesses us for obeying Him.

I would rather have 90% that's blessed, than 100% that's cursed.

Many people make a huge mistake when they assume that tithing is an option. By doing this, they place themselves in the unenviable position of being a thief who has stolen from God Himself.

This is the God who created the Earth and all that is in it. He has all power and all knowledge. Of all the people you could possibly steal from, why in the world would you choose to steal from Him? What were you thinking?

I know, there will be people who will read this book, who will see what I have to say about tithing, and will immediately want to write to me to ask a certain question, "Mark, isn't it true that tithing is not taught in the New Testament?"

My answer is, "No, it's not. As long as you just take three books out of the New Testament. If you remove two of the Gospels, and the book of Hebrews, then it's not mentioned at all. Just tear those three books out of the Bible, and you'll be fine."

You may say, "Well, Mark, that's preposterous for you to suggest that someone actually remove three books from the Bible!" It is no more ridiculous than the suggestion that something is not taught in the New Testament when it is clearly found in three different books.

My experience has taught me that usually, when someone wants to argue whether tithing is taught in the New Testament, they are not trying to justify their desire to give more than ten percent of their income to God. Typically, this is a person who wants to do as little as possible and still get by.

"THE WORD TITHE MEANS TENTH."

First of all, why in the world would you want to risk even the slightest possibility of being viewed by God as the person who stole from Him? I just don't understand that.

Secondly, if just one person came up to me and said, "Tithing is not taught in the New Testament. I am going to give 20 percent and you can't stop me.", then I'd say, "Go for it." But, as I stated previously, this is typically someone who wants to do as little as possible and still get by.

You may feel that I am being overly blunt with my explanation of tithing, but keep in mind, after you read this book, I will not be there to answer your questions. I must answer to God for the content of this book. If I am not clear in my communication with you, I could find myself guilty of negligence in my presentation of these principles. I want every person who reads this book to be blessed. And I know from personal experience that tithing is the first step towards receiving God's abundance in your life. I view tithing as the foundation of all giving. If the foundation is faulty, all other giving will be distorted as a result. So I readily admit that I am by no means vague in my presentation of this subject. But that is intentional, for the benefit of you, the reader.

Let me illustrate this with the following story by James E. Carter, from *A Sourcebook for Stewardship Sermons*:

The day the church treasurer resigned the church asked the local grain elevator manager to take the position. He agreed under two conditions:

That no treasurer's report would be given for the first year.

That no questions be asked about finances during that year.

The people were surprised but finally agreed since most of them did business with him and he was a trusted man.

At the end of the year he gave his report:

* The church indebtedness of $228,000 has been paid.

* The minister's salary had been increased by 8%.

* The Cooperative Program gifts have been paid 200%.

"I WOULD RATHER HAVE 90% THAT'S BLESSED, THAN 100% THAT'S CURSED."

* There were no outstanding bills.

* And there was a cash balance of $11,252!

Immediately the shocked congregation asked, "How did you do it? Where did the money come from?"

He quietly answered: "Most of you bring your grain to my elevator. Throughout the year I simply withheld ten percent on your behalf and gave it to the church in your name. You didn't even miss it!"

"Do you see what we could do for the Lord if we were all willing to give at least the tithe to God, who really owns it?"

And so the new treasurer had made his point.

I am often asked, "Should I tithe on my net income or my gross income?" In Exodus 22:29 (NLT), God says, **Do not hold anything back when you give me the tithe of your crops and your wine.** To me, this means that we should tithe on our gross personal income. My question is, "Do you want a net blessing or a gross blessing?"

If you have never been taught to tithe, and if this is new information to you, it may come as quite a shock, to learn that one tenth of everything you receive, belongs to God. Please keep in mind that tithe is not a suggestion. It is commanded by God. Fortunately, although there are consequences for those who do not tithe, there are even greater rewards for those who do. You should begin tithing as soon as possible to ensure God's blessings on your life.

Look at what these famous "tithers" had to say:

J. L. Kraft, head of the Kraft Cheese Corporation, who has given approximately 25% of his enormous income to Christian causes for many years, said, "The only investment I ever made which has paid consistently increasing dividends is the money I have given to the Lord."

J. D. Rockefeller said, "I never would have been able to tithe the first million dollars I ever made if I had not tithed my first salary, which was $1.50 per week."

—W. A. Criswell, *A Guidebook for Pastors*, p. 154

One of the greatest questions regarding tithing is one which is very controversial. That question is, "To whom should I give the tithe?"

In my studies of the Bible, I only find God directing us to bring the tithe into the "storehouse". In Malachi 3, the Hebrew word for "storehouse" is owtsar, meaning a depository: - armory, cellar, garner, store (-house), treasure (-house).

From what I have found regarding this, the storehouse's primary purpose was to supply the provision for the Levitical Priests. The storehouse was situated in the vicinity of the temple, where the priests ministered. The logical equivalent in New Testament times, is for us to give our tithe to the local church, to support the man or woman of God who is responsible for ministering to us, and to our families.

As in most situations, there are reasonable exceptions to this. If a person is unable to attend a local church on a regular basis, for reasons of physical incapacity or geographic limitations caused by physical distance to the church, and the inability to travel those distances on a regular basis, then it is both logical and understandable that they would tithe to the ministry which provides their "spiritual food" on a regular basis. Also, if someone is a new Christian, and does not yet have a home church, or if someone is temporarily without a home church, then I believe that it is appropriate for them to tithe to a ministry which "feeds their soul" on a regular basis, whether through television, internet ministry, audio or video media. This should only be done on a temporary basis and should not be considered a permanent situation.

If you are physically capable of attending a church, you should seek out a church which teaches the whole Bible. You should plant yourself into that church, submitting yourself to the pastoral authority within that congregation, and committing yourself to the vision of that house. Hebrews 10:11 (NJKV) says, **not forsaking the assembling of ourselves together…** We should understand the importance of association and affiliation with others of the same faith. 1 Corinthians 15:33(NIV) says, **Do not be misled: Bad company corrupts good character.** Conversely, the association with the people of God inspires and enhances Godly character in our lives.

Also, every person on Earth needs accountability in their lives. If you are not accountable to someone who has spiritual authority in your life, you are in a dangerous position, and you lack the proper protection needed for your spiritual well being. Bottom line, **"you need to be a part of a local church, submitted to the authority of the spiritual leaders in that house"**. As a part of your relationship with that church, Romans 13:7 says for you to **"give honor to whom honor is due"**. In accordance with what we have learned in regard to tithing, it is both logical and appropriate for you to tithe into the ministry of your church, supporting the spiritual leader who ministers to you on a regular basis.

As some of you may know, several years ago, God opened a tremendous door of opportunity to me. Each year, approximately half of my speaking engagements are in business conventions around the world. In many of those, I have the opportunity to share a salvation message in an optional Sunday morning worship service following the convention. At the time of the writing of this book, I have personally had the privilege of leading more than 85,000 people in a prayer to accept Christ as their Savior, at these business conventions.

"TITHING IS THE FIRST STEP TOWARDS RECEIVING GOD'S ABUNDANCE IN YOUR LIFE."

Many of those who come forward to accept Christ have no church background whatsoever, and have no idea as to what their next step should be. We do our best to follow through with these people, helping as many as possible to get planted into churches in their local areas. During the interim, until they find a home church, some of these people tithe to our ministry, on a temporary basis. That is because our ministry is feeding these new Christians, until they are "planted" into a church. But we do not encourage them to do this on a prolonged basis. In fact, we do not encourage it at all.

(If you do not have a "home church", and would like to receive assistance from our staff, in locating a good home church in your area, please feel free to email info@markgorman.com. We will gladly assist you with this, at no charge to you. We consider this a part of our ministry to the Body of Christ.)

Again, let me say that, if you are presently without a home church, I believe that it is acceptable for you to tithe into a ministry which provides spiritual food for you and your family. Once you find a home church, however, you should tithe there. I realize that by teaching this, I may be reducing the amount of money that would potentially come into our ministry from those who would gladly tithe to us on an on going basis. But I must teach the truth regardless of how that personally impacts my ministry.

"ALTHOUGH THERE ARE CONSEQUENCES FOR THOSE WHO DO NOT TITHE, THERE ARE EVEN GREATER REWARDS FOR THOSE WHO DO."

While we are on the subject of tithing, I feel that I should address one more issue, which actually does not affect most of you. This is the issue of where a minister should pay his or her tithe. In the Old Testament, God was very clear as to His wishes regarding this. All of the priests gave their tithe to the High Priest, who was their spiritual covering.

In the same way that a congregant should tithe towards the support of their spiritual covering (the pastor), we as ministers, should tithe to our spiritual covering.

I have two spiritual fathers in my life. My tithe is divided equally between these two men. They have spiritual oversight in my life and I hold myself accountable to them. They mentor me in every aspect of my ministry. I would not consider making a significant decision about the future of my ministry or my family without their input. Anytime I need their counsel, I have access to them. Except in cases where they are out of the country, I can generally speak to them within 24 hours of the time I initiate contact, and usually that same day. If you are a minister and you refer to someone as your spiritual father, but they do not truly "father" you, maintaining no contact with you, and having no personal input into your life, in my opinion, you are deceiving yourself. But, if someone is truly fathering you in ministry, it is both fitting and appropriate for you to tithe to them. To not do so, in my opinion, is an insult to their time spent with you, and the apostolic anointing on their life. (Ladies, please forgive the male reference here, but if you have a lady who is a spiritual covering to you, please make the appropriate application of this principle in your life, changing the gender references as they apply.)

By the way, I would never ask my spiritual fathers to interrupt their schedule on my behalf. If I truly want their input in my life, I will inconvenience myself and augment my schedule to enable me to have time with them. I respect their time and their anointing, and I honor them, not only with my tithe, but also with my actions.

During the service Monday night, you told the story from the 1950's about how that woman took a step of faith. This was something I had never done before. I tithe very little because I have very little to give, or so that was my excuse. I have planted $5 in your ministry. It was all I could spare. Tuesday, I added up all the bills, rent, etc., of which all is due by Sunday, that came to a total of $920.00. I figured I would make at least $700 this weekend at work. I was coming up short, and I had no idea what I was going to do. Wednesday, my aunt called and said that I had some mail waiting at her house. She added that I had finally received a child support check from my son's father. Out of total shock, I asked her to please open it up and tell me how much it was for. As tears ran down my face, she replied, "$221.00." See I was exactly $220 short for my bills this month. The check was for one dollar over what I needed. The first thing I thought of was the seed I had planted and that I was reaping from what I sowed. I never believed all of that stuff before, sowing, tithing, etc. All I could do was cry. God made a believer out of me.
[D. S. FROM LOUISIANA]

Your talk on the 4 types of giving has really touched me. I started going to a new Christian Church that is a church you would approve of. They believe in the whole Bible and introduced the biblical principle of tithing. I now tithe all my checks I receive from my business and any other income I receive. It has been tough but in this last month I have really seen my business take off. I am 19 years old, my dad has been involved in the business for 4 years, and for about a year I have really been plugged into building my own future. Like I mentioned before, like most people I am not a natural giver, but after you spoke I felt a burden on my heart from God to give and write this note.
[S. W. OF MICHIGAN]

We thoroughly enjoyed the morning worship and the ministry you both had to married couples such as ourselves during the last business conference in Florida. We love to give and the thought of being able to support y'all was an exciting way of saying thank you for all the times you have blessed us through word and tape. We stood to be counted among those who would support what God is doing through your ministry. After returning to Tampa, I checked our stock portfolio only to see it had risen in value over $1,400.00. I was amazed and thankful.

[K. V. OF FLORIDA]

CHAPTER 5

THE FOUR TYPES OF GIVING
- FIRSTFRUITS -

The second type of giving taught in the Bible is firstfruits. Of the four types of giving, only tithe and firstfruits are commanded by God. Deuteronomy 18:4 (NKJV) says, "**The firstfruits of your grain and your new wine and your oil, and the first of the fleece of your sheep, you shall give him**".

The firstfruit is actually the first "taste" of any increase you receive, whether it is a raise, a bonus, or any other additional source of income. Historically the first yield of your crops and the first born of your herds and flocks were all considered "firstfruits" and therefore holy unto the Lord. In offering them without hesitation and with thanksgiving to God, you acknowledged His sovereignty, and your position as stewards. In other words, we have nothing—including ourselves—which didn't come from God, and thus everything we have ultimately belongs to God. Meanwhile, scripture also makes it clear that the increase of your possessions is also considered as "firstfruits" that is to be holy unto God.

Proverbs 3:9-10 (NIV) "**Honor the LORD with your wealth, with the firstfruits of all your crops; then your barns will be filled to overflowing, and your vats will brim over with new wine**".

Basically anytime you receive increase in your life, the first "taste" belongs to God. For example, if your received a raise on your job which resulted in an additional $50 per week, and if you were paid every two weeks, this means that there would be an additional $100 in your first paycheck following the raise. That entire amount should be given to God. You may say, "But I need that extra money!" You've been living without it until now. By doing without it for one more pay period, you are showing your gratitude to God for His blessing, and ensuring more blessings in the future.

I once read a story about two young boys whose grandfather gave each of them a box of chocolates. After taking his box into his bedroom, the first boy quickly opened it, and was soon covered in a chocolate mess, as he consumed the entire box in one sitting. The other boy, however, remained in the room with his grandfather. He gently opened the box, and after removing the thin sheet of wax paper which covered the candies, he lifted the box to his grandfather and said, "Grandpa, thank you for my chocolates. Here, why don't you have the first piece?"

If you receive an increase in your life and do not honor God with that increase, ask yourself, what must He think you are feeling about that increase? Either you are ungrateful for what He has done in your life, or you were not impressed with the blessing He gave you. In either case, is there a motivation for Him to repeat the blessing in the future?

Again, notice that, although God requires the firstfruits from us, He promises to bless us for giving Him His property. What a generous God! He could simply threaten to punish us if we do not give to Him what is rightfully His.

Ezekiel 44:30 (NIV) **"The best of all the firstfruits and of all your special gifts will belong to the priests. You are to give them the first portion of your ground meal so that a blessing may rest on your household"**.

My cousin, Dwayne works with me, in our ministry. In fact, at the time of the writing of this book, he and his wife, Deanna have worked for our ministry for approximately five years. Last year, Dwayne received a substantial raise in pay.

"THE FIRSTFUIT IS ACTUALLY THE FIRST "TASTE" OF ANY INCREASE YOU RECEIVE, WHETHER IT IS A RAISE, BONUS, OR ANY OTHER ADDITIONAL SOURCE OF INCOME."

(I do not pay people based on the amount of income that our ministry receives or based upon their personal needs. I feel that as a good steward, I should pay people based on one thing only; I pay the job, and not the person. If you pay people based on their needs, that is welfare. God's Word teaches us that people should be paid based on job performance, as is illustrated in the parable of the talents. Matthew 25:14-30)

About a week after he had received his first paycheck, which reflected the raise, Dwayne came to me. With a smile on his face, he said, "When I got that first paycheck, containing the raise, I was so excited! Then I remembered what you teach about firstfruits. I knew what I had to do. Deanna and I prayed about it and we felt that, instead of giving the firstfruits in the church offering, we should give it personally to our pastor and his wife. When we handed it to them, by the look on their faces, I knew that we had done the right thing."

Since that time, Dwayne and Deanna have received blessing after blessing of God's abundance. Recently, I had the privilege of praying with them, to dedicate their new home to God. It's the first house they have ever owned. In spite of the additional costs of being a homeowner, they are still more blessed financially than they have ever been before.

Because our ministry is a federally recognized non-profit corporation, the same as a church, the ministry must be governed by a board of directors. This means that I have no say in the amount of my salary. It is determined exclusively by the board of directors of the non-profit corporation. This past December, the board voted to give me a raise in pay.

When Gina and I received the first paycheck which contained our increase, we knew that we must give the entire increase to God as our firstfruits. We prayed and asked God how we should give it. The Lord spoke to us and said that one fourth should go to our pastors, one fourth to each of my spiritual fathers, and one fourth to a pastor, who God directed us to.

As you will note, Ezekiel 44:30 says that we are to give the firstfruits to "the priests". The modern day equivalent of the Old Testament priests, would be anyone in five-fold ministry: Apostles, Prophets, Evangelists, Pastors, and Teachers. I believe that, as long as you are led by the Spirit, it is appropriate to give firstfruits to anyone who is in full-time, five-fold ministry.

Again, there will probably be those who will ask if firstfruits applies to us today, since this was introduced in the Old Testament. Romans 11:16 (NIV) says, **"If the part of the dough offered as firstfruits is holy, then the whole batch is holy; if the root is holy, so are the branches".**

This helps us to see that the giving of firstfruits was still practiced in the New Testament, even after Jesus had ascended into Heaven, following His resurrection. We know this because the book of Romans was written by the Apostle Paul, who did not come to Christ until after Jesus' death, resurrection, and ascension.

As I stated in the previous chapter on tithes, if there is even the slightest question in your mind, why take the chance? Why would you even risk having "unpaid debt" with God? Besides, when we do give Him the firstfruits of our increase, He has promised that our barns will be filled to overflowing, and our vats will brim over with new wine, signifying His promise of more increase to come in the future.

Thank you for the two-part message on the four types of giving – I have been in disobedience to God until now and praise him for the incredible way he led me to your ministry. I first heard you, Mark, I was led to recommit my life to Jesus at a business convention years ago. Thank you.
[M. S. OF NOVA SCOTIA]

I had the pleasure of hearing you speak on Father's Day and the following Wednesday as well. At the end of your Wednesday message you asked any who had a need to please stand. Typically I would not have stood but something made me just about jump to my feet. To make a long story short you said you expected 3 miracles. The only part I had a problem with us is that I didn't know if I had enough faith or if I even knew what faith really was!! The following Sunday the pastor spoke about faith and belief, this clarified it and I new I would get my miracles. Just nine days after you spoke my wife's grandmother sent us a check for $1,000.00. We also did get the other two miracles.
[D. W. OF NEW YORK]

Within the last two months I wrote a letter to you requesting prayer for our business. We are one of your 300. Things were really bad and we (my husband, my daughter, her husband and myself...are in business together) were all very discouraged. Our business wasn't making it and therefore our personal finances were also in a mess. It was hard for us to understand, because we try very hard to serve the Lord and follow what he wants us to do. We are also givers. Anyway, to make a long story short...I felt like God wanted us to raise our prices (we hadn't in several years in fear because we were afraid we wouldn't get the jobs if we went any higher in our prices, but what we were charging wouldn't pay our bills). We prayed about it and raised our prices. We also started giving more than we already were. The jobs started coming in (and only a few complained about our higher prices...they left, but came back and hired us after looking elsewhere).

We now have an ABUNDANCE of work lined up. Enough money has come in that we are current in payroll and even received back payroll we were owed from the company. PRAISE GOD!!!
[B. G. OF COLORADO]

CHAPTER 6

∽◉◠

The Four Types Of Giving
- Alms -

The third type of giving taught in the Bible is alms. In the original Greek, the word alms is eleé mosuné. By definition, this means generosity that is motivated by compassion or sympathy towards the poor.

Acts 3:2-3 (NKJV) states, "**And a certain man lame from his mother's womb was carried, whom they laid daily at the gate of the temple which is called Beautiful, to ask alms from those who entered the temple; who, seeing Peter and John about to go into the temple, asked for alms**".

This is an excellent example of the function of alms, and the motivation for giving alms.

Of the four types of giving taught in the Bible, alms is the only one which is not given to God, but to man. Keep in mind, God is not poor and we do not need to feel sorry for Him. Therefore, we do not give alms to God – only to people.

In fact, the Bible cautions us to maintain a level of secrecy regarding the giving of alms. Matthew 6:1-4 (NRSV) says, "**Beware of practicing your piety before others in order to be seen by them; for then you have no reward from your Father in heaven. So whenever you give alms, do not sound a trumpet before you, as the hypocrites do in the synagogues and in the streets, so that they may be praised by others. Truly I tell you, they have received their reward. But when you give alms, do not let your left hand know what your right hand is doing, so that your alms may be done in secret; and your Father who sees in secret will reward you**".

Many people have misinterpreted the meaning of this passage, and have assumed that we are to maintain this same level of secrecy regarding all of our giving, when the Bible actually teaches just the opposite.

In one passage in the New Testament, we find Jesus and His disciples standing near the offering receptacle observing the amount given by each person. Were it not for their curiosity about the giving of others, we would have no record of the story of "the widow's mite". In that story, Jesus taught the disciples a lesson by drawing a comparison between the widow's offering and what others had given. In this story, He made it obvious that God looks more closely at the amount of sacrifice than the "dollar amount".

In Luke 21: 3-4, we find Jesus' words, **"Truly I say to you that this poor widow has put in more than all; for all these out of their abundance have put in offerings for God, but she out of her poverty put in all the livelihood that she had"**.

All of this leads us back to the fact that when Jesus said that we should not tell anyone what we have given, He was speaking only of alms and not in regard to the other three types of giving.

Why was it so important for Him to make this stipulation? Think about it; if you had learned that someone could not pay their rent, and you were moved with sympathy to help them, which resulted in you giving them some money, wouldn't it be humiliating for them if you told everyone else what you had done? I believe His purpose in admonishing us in this way was to prevent us from devastating someone emotionally, who is already in financial need.

— ⌒ —

"ALMS IS THE ONLY TYPE OF GIVING WHICH IS NOT GIVEN TO GOD, BUT TO MAN."

I could cite other references in the Bible in which attention was drawn to the amount given in an offering such as the story of Ananias and Sapphira in the book of Acts.

Suffice to stay that God does not teach us to keep all of our giving a secret. Rather, He admonishes us to protect the dignity of those in crisis, who need our assistance.

There are many references in the Bible to the fact that God wants us to be generous towards the poor.

Proverbs 14:21 (NLT) **"It is sin to despise one's neighbors; blessed are those who help the poor"**. This means that if your neighbor is in need, and you are unmoved by their situation, you will eventually suffer the consequence of this attitude. But, if you reach out to help them in their time of need, you will be blessed.

Proverbs 19:17 (NKJV) **"He who has pity on the poor lends to the LORD, And He will pay back what he has given"**. This passage helps us to understand the promise of blessing for those who give alms. Specifically, God will reimburse you for whatever you give to the poor.

Proverbs 21:13 (NLT) **"Those who shut their ears to the cries of the poor will be ignored in their own time of need"**.

Proverbs 22:9 (NRSV) **"Those who are generous are blessed, for they share their bread with the poor"**.

Proverbs 28:27 (NLT) **"Whoever gives to the poor will lack nothing. But a curse will come upon those who close their eyes to poverty"**.

I think it is obvious that God is pleased with those who have a generous heart towards the poor, and He will reward them accordingly.

I just wanted to let you know I am grateful I donated to your ministry. God had me redo the past two year's tax returns and I got money back from them. I also got an extra $700.00 from a 401k from a job that downsized. Since then I have already gotten over $1000.00 unexpectedly.
[M. S. OF WASHINGTON]

I recently received an annual bonus at my job. Thank you once again for the ministry you extend through your tapes which continues to minister to me on a daily basis.
[M. H. OF NOVA SCOTIA]

Recently I was one who pledged $1000.00 in seed faith. Now, as it happens, I had been on an injury leave and I wasn't getting well enough to go back to work, as it is a very physical job. I had been told that my knees weren't worth much in the scheme of disability compensations and that I should only expect $2,000.00 - $3,000.00. I am very pleased to tell you that the final pay off to me was a little more than twice what I had been told. Yea!!
[B. S. OF COLORADO]

CHAPTER 7

∽≈✍

THE FOUR TYPES OF GIVING
- SEED -

The fourth type of giving taught in the Bible is seed.

2 Corinthians 9:6-11 (NIV) Remember this: "**Whoever sows sparingly will also reap sparingly, and whoever sows generously will also reap generously. Each man should give what he has decided in his heart to give, not reluctantly or under compulsion, for God loves a cheerful giver. And God is able to make all grace abound to you, so that in all things at all times, having all that you need, you will abound in every good work. As it is written: "He has scattered abroad his gifts to the poor; his righteousness endures forever." Now he who supplies seed to the sower and bread for food will also supply and increase your store of seed and will enlarge the harvest of your righteousness. You will be made rich in every way so that you can be generous on every occasion, and through us your generosity will result in thanksgiving to God".**

Several years ago, Gina and I were going through the worst financial crisis we had ever faced. I tell people that we were "below broke". It really was bad. What's worse is, we didn't see a way out. It's one thing to be in a bad situation, but when you can't see the "light at the end of the tunnel", it can be depressing and overwhelming.

Like so many other Christians, in my time of crisis, I cried out to God, and asked Him for help with our finances. His reply was somewhat shocking.

Instead of telling me that help was on the way, He said that I should "plant my way out of poverty". I said, "But God, I'm already tithing."

He then informed me of something which I had not previously understood. He told me that the tithe is not seed, and that seed planting starts at 11%, after the tithe. (Keep in mind, this was many years ago. Like many other Christians, I assumed that all giving was the same, not understanding what I'm teaching now, that there are actually four types of giving.)

The Bible often speaks of this type of giving as offerings. It is interesting to note that, of the four types of giving taught in the Bible, this is the only one which involves you giving your money to God. Think about it: the tithe is the Lord's – it's already His property before you give it to Him. The firstfruits belong to Him. When you give alms, it is voluntary on your part, but you are not giving it to Him. Remember, alms is given out of sympathy, and is given to people who are in need, not to God. When you plant financial seed, you are "offering" God something that is yours.

Now, back to our story; when I understood the difference between tithe and seed, I realized what we needed to do. Regardless of our financial circumstances at the time, I knew we needed to get some seed in the ground. Gina and I prayed and made a decision to start sowing an extra 10% of the total ministry income into the Kingdom of God. Our tithes were separate. This is different from our tithes.

You may ask, "If the finances were so bad, where did you get the money to sow?"

Well, basically, I made some of our creditors wait a little longer until we could put some seed in the ground. Also, we "cut back" on every expense possible in order to have more to sow.

You may say, "Well, that's irresponsible, for you to make the creditors wait for you to pay them."

Actually, what I find to be ridiculous are people who eat all of their seed, and still look for a harvest. We knew that if we didn't get some seed into the ground, we would never have a harvest.

Remember this; God does not owe you a harvest just because you are saved. Get rid of that welfare mentality, which causes people to think that God owes them a financial blessing just because they have a need.

As I have already stated, 2 Corinthians 9:10 says, "**God gives seed to the sower**". It doesn't say that He gives seed to the needy, the poor, the widow, the orphan, or even the righteous. He only gives seed to the sower.

Why? Because He doesn't want the seed to be wasted. He knows that only a sower would use the seed properly. If you want God to put seed into your hand, you must first develop the heart of a sower. You become a sower in your heart before you ever sow with your hand. God is looking for people with the heart of a sower so He can put seed into their hands.

When Gina and I began sowing the seed, an extra 10% of our ministry's income, in that first year, the income doubled.

We still sow more than 10% of our ministry's income every year. At the end of last year, the ministry's annual income was more than 20 times what it was when we first started sowing seed many years ago. Sowing and reaping really does work.

When I was just beginning to learn some of these financial principles, God used some friends of ours to teach me a valuable lesson. I was home, between speaking engagements, and had taken my family to our home church on the Wednesday night. (In case you are not familiar with my ministry, I do not pastor a church. We have a home church in New Orleans, which we attend when we are home.)

As we were driving home from church that Wednesday evening, Gina looked at me and said, "Guess what Jerry and Gwen gave me tonight." There was a frustrated look on her face – almost irritated. I had no idea what they could have given her that would have caused such strong feelings, so I asked.

She replied, "They gave me $100!"

Now, most people would be a little happier than that after receiving $100. But as soon as I learned this, I too, was upset. Why? Because we both knew that Jerry and Gwen did not have that kind of money, to be giving $100 to anyone.

I immediately declared, "There is no way that they can afford to do that! Why didn't you give it back?"

"I tried!", she said. "They claimed that God told them to."

"That's ridiculous! God knows that they can not afford to give that kind of money." I remarked. "Did they give you cash or a check?" She said that they'd given her a check.

My "solution" was that we would not deposit the check.

After hearing my brilliant idea, Gina asked how long we would wait before doing something with the check.

I said, "I don't know. Let me pray about it. I need to hear from God."

A couple of weeks later, I was up early one morning praying. It was about 5:30 in the morning, and the sun was just starting to appear on the horizon. Its golden rays glistening on the water, as I walked alongside a lake, near our home. (I find that it is easier for me to hear God, and to feel close to Him, when I am near nature. When Jesus could choose His places of prayer, He chose mountains, desserts, and gardens. In fact, to write this book, I drove more than three hours from our home, in New Orleans, to find a place on the beach where I could be inspired as I look out at the waves, rolling onto the shore.)

As I communed with God, He spoke to me and said, "You can give the money back."

This took me completely by surprise. I had no idea what He was talking about, so I asked Him to help me understand what He meant.

He then said, "Jerry and Gwen; you can give the money back."

I was so excited! Now I had heard from God. I could go to them and say, "Thus saith the Lord. Taketh it backeth." (When someone says something in King James English, doesn't it seem more authoritative? Ha!)

Just as I was preparing to do a "victory dance", God continued speaking and said, "But if you give it back, you will only be giving them seed, and they don't need seed, they need a harvest." (You may recall that He said something similar to me in Ivory Coast, Africa when I met Constance. Actually, this was my first time to learn that principle, long before I met Constance.)

Immediately after hearing this word from the Lord, I ran to my car and drove straight home. Upon entering our home, I walked straight to our bedroom and woke Gina at about 6 am. I franticly said, "Where's that check? We've got to get that seed in the ground."

She was a bit disoriented at first, and then looked at me through squinted eyes and asked, "What are you talking about?"

I said, "The check from Jerry and Gwen. God just spoke to me, and told me that we have to deposit that check so their seed can be planted, and they can get a harvest."

She said, "It's in my purse, but what's the hurry?"

I suddenly realized that the bank didn't open until 9 am, so I didn't need to be quite so urgent about this, at that moment. (I'm so bright sometimes!) Gina eventually located the check in her purse. We held it in our hands and prayed for God to bring harvest into Jerry and Gwen's life, before Gina deposited it into the ministry checking account later that day.

About three or four months later, we were at church again on a Wednesday night, when I was home between ministry trips. As we were pulling into a parking space, I heard someone behind me honking repeatedly. I thought, "Who in the world can that be? What's the big hurry?" (I hate it when people drive like me. That is so rude.)

First, you need to know something: as long as I had known them, Jerry and Gwen had driven what I call "miracle cars". Do you know the kind of car I am talking about? It's a miracle that is starts – it's a miracle that it runs - and it's a miracle that it stops. It's just a miracle all the way around. Ha!

In the rearview mirror, I could see that it was someone in a brand new Dodge Intrepid. When we got out of the car and began walking to the church, we walked over to see who had been honking at us. It was Jerry and Gwen in the first new car they had ever owned. They wanted us to see their harvest.

After rejoicing with them over God's provision, Gina and I turned to walk into the church. As we were walking up the church steps, God spoke to me and said, "Now, which do you think they would rather have: the $100 seed, or the new car?"

It was obvious what He was teaching me. All I could say was, "Thanks for rubbing it in. I got the message."

I can just picture someone asking, "If they sowed $100 seed and got an Intrepid, how much for a Mercedes?" It doesn't work that way.

If anyone tells you that, if you sow a specific seed, a particular harvest will result, don't believe them. All we can do is what the farmer does: he sows as much as he can, in faith, and waits for God's increase.

Also, I do not believe that our ministry was the only one they had planted seed in, during that period of several months prior to receiving their new car. But I do know that God's Word is true and that sowing and reaping works.

Let me give you another example. Many years ago, our family traveled with me in ministry, driving from church to church in a mini-van. There came a point when I knew that we needed a larger vehicle, not only for additional interior space for long trips, but also a larger engine to tow a cargo trailer with sound equipment, teaching tapes, etc.

As I began to pray, asking God for a full-size van, God spoke to me. He said, "Plant a van."

I asked, "How do you plant a van?"

The Lord began to teach me that, when a farmer sows a seed, he is not sowing the entire plant which he expects in his harvest, but he is sowing a specific seed which will produce the desired return. For example, if a farmer wishes to harvest watermelons, he does not go into the field planting entire watermelons, but he does plant a specific type of seed which he knows will produce watermelons in its harvest.

Gina and I began to sow financial seeds, naming them as "seed for a van". We planted these seeds for several months, surrounding them with prayer and faith for a harvest.

After a few months of planting, God spoke to my heart and told me that it was time to "harvest our van". We began visiting dealership after dealership in the New Orleans area, looking at numerous vans. Some of them had engines which were too small for the type of towing we needed to do, or their suspension was not heavy enough to sustain the prolonged towing of a trailer. Others were overly extravagant with ridiculous price tags.

"GOD IS LOOKING FOR PEOPLE WITH THE HEART OF A SOWER, SO HE CAN PUT SEED INTO THEIR HANDS."

After several days of looking, we found ourselves at an auto dealership on the other side of the Mississippi River, in a suburb of New Orleans.

I don't know how many vans I had looked at that day, but I turned to Gina and said, "I've had it! There's nothing here for us. Let's go home."

Gina said, "But there are a lot more vans over there on the other side of the dealership."

But I remarked, "I already told you, I don't think there is anything for us. Let's go home."

Proverbs 10:5 (NIV) says, **"He who gathers crops in summer is a wise son, but he who sleeps during harvest is a disgraceful son"**.

I was "sleeping through" my own harvest. Thank God, Gina was awake!

She looked at me and said, "Well, it wouldn't hurt to look!"

With a sigh of frustration, I turned to walk with her, and our children to the other side of the dealership lot, to look at even more vans. As we walked along looking at the different models available, one van stood out above the rest. It was beautiful.

It was black with tan and gold stripes. It had a raised roof for extra room inside. There were leather seats throughout, with a sofa in the rear. There was an electric button on the wall, which could be pushed, to turn the sofa into a bed. The van came with a TV, VCR, two separate stereo systems, front and rear air conditioners, a large heavy-duty engine, a suspension which was rated for towing, a leather steering wheel, cruise control, and many other extras. We were all amazed at the amenities this van offered.

Gina said, "Why don't you go inside and ask how much this van would cost."

I replied, "Are you serious? Look at this van! There are so many features; there is no way we could afford it!"

Gina said, "Well, it wouldn't hurt to ask." (Thank God even though I was sleeping through my harvest, Gina was awake.)

As I walked into the dealership, I inquired about the van. One of the managers said. "Oh, you mean last year's model?"

I said, "What?"

He said, "Oh yes, that's the only van from last year which hasn't sold. It has so many added features; I have no idea why it didn't sell. We've been hoping that someone would want it. The dealership is anxious to get it off of the lot. I'll bet they'd make you a really good deal if you buy that one."

Now, in retrospect, I know why that van hadn't sold. That was my van! It was my harvest. We had planted that van!

The sales manager returned, and said that the dealership was prepared to take all of their profits out of the van, if we would just buy it that day. They even took out the factory hold-back. Then he informed us that there was an additional $1500 rebate on that particular van. It was almost as if they were paying us to take it!

When all was said and done, we purchased a van which retailed for $38,000, for less than $23,000. If you have purchased a vehicle recently, you will know that this is not normal.

Keep in mind, this occurred in the early stages of our "education" in regard to sowing and reaping. God used this to teach us a valuable lesson about "naming our seed".

After signing the papers for the purchase of the van, we came outside to drive it home for the first time. When we walked out of the dealership there was a lady in our new van! She was looking around, and asked, "How much is this van?"

I said, "This van is sold."

"DON'T SLEEP THROUGH YOUR HARVEST."

She replied, "But I just want to know how much it is."

I said, "It's doesn't matter how much it is, because it's not for sale."

Do you realize that if Gina had not been there, we would have missed our harvest. I would have slept right through it. Remember, I was ready to leave and go home, before we saw this van.

Don't sleep through your harvest.

Genesis 8:22 (NKJV) "**While the earth remains, Seedtime and harvest, …Shall not cease**".

Our previous "seeds" have had bountiful, exciting and heart filled harvests! Our company has enjoyed the harvest of 2 new, very nice work vans and the adding of another employee. Our family has the pleasure to announce that my husband's father has finally accepted the Lord as his Savior full-heartedly! My husband has prayed for his father since he was 7 years old. There are other day to day blessings, too numerous to count. The Lord is ever present in our lives.
[C. M. OF COLORADO]

During one of your business conferences, you and I came into agreement about a seed offering my wife and I desired to sow into your ministry. As you know, we were believing God to hasten the sale of a van we owned. We placed an advertisement in the newspaper Sunday. We received only one call about the van. The man came and drove it. He then gave us what we wanted for the van. We sowed a seed of $100.00 believing for the sale to generate a $1000.00 seed – a seed sown to break the back of poverty. The van sold and our prayer was answered. Please find a check enclosed for your ministry of $1000.00.
[T. B. OF GEORGIA]

We have been blessed abundantly since we planted our $5000.00 seed with your ministry. We have had a three-fold increase in our income. Praise God! His Word is so true! It has been tested over and over again and is ALWAYS proven true! Glory to God!
[J. A. FROM FLORIDA]

∽ౖ

CHAPTER 8

THE FOUR TYPES OF GIVING
- EXPLAINED -

It is interesting to note that most Christians never tithe, they never give firstfruits, and they never sow seed. They only give alms.

You may ask, "Why do you say that?"

To understand this, you must look at the motivation behind our giving. First, let's take a look at tithing. God is very clear in what He says about tithing. In Malachi chapter 3, He states that a person who does not tithe is a thief. By this, we understand that the tithe is God's property, otherwise, how could a person be considered a thief if they keep the tithe.

Again, there may be some, who are "holding out" to argue their belief, that tithing was only for the Old Testament, and not for us today. In response, I would refer them to: Hebrews 13:8 (NKJV) **"Jesus Christ is the same yesterday and today and forever"**.

If God said that the tithe was His, in Old Testament times, I see no reason that He would change His feelings about that now.

Based on this fact, the motivation for tithing is obedience. When you tithe, you are simply obeying God. As I see it, you're not generous until you hit 11%, and you're not honest 'til you hit 10%. (I've never been accused of being vague.)

Now, let us look at firstfruits. There are 31 references to firstfruits in the Bible. This alone should testify to the fact that God feels strongly about the firstfruits and that they are His property.

In addition, Exodus 34:26 (NKJV) says, **The first of the firstfruits of your land you shall bring to the house of the Lord your God...**

This, too, makes it clear that the firstfruits is also God's property.

Therefore, the motivation for giving firstfruits is also obedience.

Because alms are given to the poor, the obvious motivation for giving alms is sympathy.

When we sow seed as an offering, the motivation is faith. Even a farmer who does not know God, must exercise faith to take something in his hand and say, "I want more of this, so I am going to bury it under that dirt, and believe for it to multiply."

TYPE OF GIVING		MOTIVATION
TITHE	---------▸--------	OBEDIENCE
FIRSTFRUITS	---------▸--------	OBEDIENCE
ALMS	---------▸--------	SYMPATHY
SEED	---------▸--------	FAITH

Now, let's look at what motivates most Christian's to give:

Many people will walk into a church and notice that the walls need to be painted, the carpet needs to be replaced, and the pastor is wearing old, worn-out clothes, and driving an old, run-down car. When they see this, many will say, "Bless their hearts, they need some help. Let's give our tithe here."

"YOU'RE NOT GENEROUS UNTIL YOU HIT 11%, AND YOU'RE NOT HONEST 'TIL YOU HIT 10%."

What is motivating them to give? It's obviously sympathy. Although they are giving 10% of their income, it is not tithe, because it is not motivated by obedience. Instead, because their giving is motivated by sympathy, they are obviously giving alms.

It is very important for us to understand this because many people think that the fact that they are giving 10% of their income, automatically means that it is tithe. When, in reality, because they are motivated by sympathy, they are giving alms. This means that they are not giving to God, but to man.

You may say, "How can you say that?" Let me answer your question, with a question: Have you ever felt sorry for God? If you do not have sympathy for God and your offering is motivated by sympathy, then you must ask yourself to whom are you giving? You are obviously motivated by feelings of pity for the pastor and the church.

That same person may attend another church which is beautifully decorated with lovely chandeliers and luxurious carpet. The pastor may wear fine clothing, driving a brand new car. They may look at this church and say, "Well, they're doing fine without us. They don't need our tithe. Let's give our tithe somewhere else, where they need it."

Again, as with the previous scenario, this person's giving is motivated by sympathy, not by obedience. Therefore, they are not giving tithe, but alms.

You may ask, "What's the big deal? As long as I am giving, what does it matter whether I am giving tithe or alms."

First, God has made it very clear that the tithe is His property. If you are not tithing, then He calls you a thief. I don't know about you, but I don't want God to view me as a thief, particularly one who has stolen His property. Secondly, let's take a look at the reward for each type of giving.

God says that He will reward the tither by doing two things: He will open the windows of Heaven to pour out a blessing which is more than you can hold, and He will rebuke the devourer for your sake.

For the giving of firstfruits, the reward is that your barns will be filled to overflowing, and your vats will brim over with new wine.

The reward for giving alms is actually the least of all four. Why?

Because alms are not given to God, but to man. Therefore, God says that when we give alms, we can claim the promise found in Proverbs 19:17 (NKJV) **He who has pity on the poor lends to the LORD, And He will pay back what he has given.**

Basically this means that the reward for giving alms is that you will be reimbursed. If you give the poor a dollar, God will give you a dollar. I tell people that the reward for alms is dollar for dollar.

Seed gives the greatest return of all four. Think about it: How many peaches do you get from a peach seed? No one knows. There's no way you can put a number on that. How many apples do you get from an apple seed? Again, there is no way to calculate that number, because the harvest goes on for year after year.

Some people who realize that seed has the greatest return will try to opt for sowing seed first. But, in actuality, your seed sowing begins at 11%, after the tithe.

Also, those who try to sow seed without giving tithe will find that, although they receive a generous harvest, they will soon lose it, because the "devourer" is not being rebuked on their behalf.

TYPE OF GIVING	MOTIVATION	REWARD
TITHE	OBEDIENCE	OPEN HEAVEN S WINDOWS REBUKE DEVOURER
FIRSTFRUITS	OBEDIENCE	BARNS FILLED TO OVERFLOWING VATS BRIM OVER WITH WINE
ALMS	SYMPATHY	REIMBURSEMENT DOLLAR FOR DOLLAR
SEED	FAITH	HARVEST - MULTIPLICATION THE LARGEST RETURN OF ALL

Many Christians have a cynical attitude towards prosperity and particularly sowing and reaping. Because of their own experience, they believe that the principles I am teaching do not actually work.

In reality, this is usually caused by the fact that they only give when they are moved with compassion and sympathy for a person or a ministry. This means that they only give alms, resulting in the least of all returns: reimbursement – dollar for dollar. This is why most Christians never get ahead in their finances – because they don't give unless they "feel sorry for someone".

I was like that. Growing up in church, with my father as the pastor, I saw many visiting ministries in our pulpit. Sometimes, my dad would have a visiting ministry for whom I felt sorry. Maybe their clothing was out of date and worn-out. Perhaps their car looked as if it barely made it down the street. When I saw such people in the pulpit, I was moved with compassion and sympathy. I would say to myself, "Bless their heart. I want to help them. I'm going to give something to bless their ministry."

Was I sowing seed? Obviously not. What was the motivation for my giving? It was sympathy. Therefore, what was I giving? Alms. And what was my return on that giving? Reimbursement - dollar for dollar.

My father would have other visiting ministries in the church, who drove nicer cars than I had and wore nicer clothing than I wore. Did I feel sorry for them? Absolutely not.

I would look at them and say to myself, "Bless God, they're doing OK without me. They don't need my money. I'm not giving anything to them."

Even if I would have given to that ministry, would I have been giving seed? No, I would have been giving alms and again, my return would have been reimbursement - dollar for dollar.

To me, this is one of the most important chapters in the entire book, because it helps to give perspective to our giving and to the rewards for that giving, or the lack thereof. I'm sure that many of you, as you have read the last few

> "THE MOTIVATION FOR GIVING ALMS IS SYMPATHY."

paragraphs, are beginning to understand why you are not getting ahead in your finances.

As I have learned God's principles for financial abundance, I have begun to understand with greater clarity, not only the motivation for my giving, but also the expected results. This has also helped me to understand what type of giving I must do, when I need increase.

First, I MUST be a tither. This is not an option. It is an absolute must. This will open the windows of heaven to pour out blessing, and cause the devourer to be rebuked.

Second, I must ensure that every time there is increase in my life, the first taste (firstfruits) goes to God. This will guarantee more increase in the future.

Third, for the greatest increase, I must look for soil (a ministry) which is already producing the kind of harvest that I want in my life, and plant generous seed there.

The practice of these three principles has resulted in prosperity and abundance in my own life and my ministry, enabling me to give alms to those in need, when God directs me to help them.

It amazes me, when I see that farmers are looking for "rich soil", while Christians are looking for "poor preachers". You may ask, "Mark, does this mean that you do not give to people and ministries who are in need?" No, it does not mean that at all. I give very generously to many ministries and people for whom I feel compassion and sympathy. But I do not expect a harvest in return, because I know that I am giving alms. Therefore, I know that when I give to a needy person, I will only be reimbursed - dollar for dollar. The reason I do not elaborate on this is simply that God tell us in His Word that we should not tell others what we are giving in regard to alms.

> "WHEN WE SOW SEED AS AN OFFERING, THE MOTIVATION IS FAITH."

I can imagine that there will be those who read this book, who have "needy ministries". Their reaction may be similar to that of many people who have heard me in person. I have no idea how many people have approached me after hearing me teach on giving, and hearing that my number one dream is to give at least a million dollars to missions. Numerous people have handed me brochures regarding their ministry asking that I add them to my list of ministries which I support, and others have e-mailed or written to me, asking the same.

There are only two reasons why I support a "needy ministry":

1) I am in relationship with that ministry, or with another ministry to whom they relate. (I am very "big" on relationships, and I believe that all ministry should be based on relationship - not on association or affiliation. We don't have time to get into that now - perhaps, in a future book.)

2) If God speaks to me about a specific ministry and about their needy cause, I will gladly obey Him because He is the One Who provides everything I have.

But I can tell you now, that if God does not speak to me about supporting a needy ministry with alms, or if I am not in relationship with their "spiritual covering", there is little chance that I will support that particular ministry. I would encourage you to use similar discernment in your giving of alms. Don't support a ministry simply because they have a need. There may be a good reason why they are needy. In fact, it may be that God has "cut off" His supply to that ministry, because they are not fulfilling His purpose.

Now, let me talk to the pastors who are reading this book. How many times have we heard pastors say, at offering time, "Please give generously because the need is great."

Pastor, think about this. When you appeal to your congregation to give based on the need, you are appealing to their sympathy.

"IT AMAZES ME, WHEN I SEE THAT FARMERS ARE LOOKING FOR "RICH SOIL", WHILE CHRISTIANS ARE LOOKING FOR "POOR PREACHERS".

Even if they give as a result of your "needy plea", what are they giving? Since they would be motivated by sympathy, they would be giving alms. This means that their return on that offering would be merely a reimbursement - dollar for dollar.

When I speak at churches, in sharing with the people about the offering, I NEVER ask them to give to our ministry. In my opinion, if our ministry is good soil, they will want to give. If after hearing me, they are not motivated to give to our ministry, and they do not believe that it is good soil, then they should not give.

I NEVER appeal to people's sympathy in regard to the offering for our ministry. Why? (There are many preachers who raise lots of money appealing to people's sympathy.) I know that, even if they give to our ministry out of sympathy, they will never "get ahead" because they will only be reimbursed.

When I share before our offerings, I am always honest with the congregation. I tell them clearly that God has blessed and prospered us, and that they should NOT give out of sympathy. I explain that they should only give if they believe that our ministry is good soil, and if they want to receive the same kind of harvest in their lives, that we have in our ministry.

Pastors, let me help you. When you talk to your people about giving, especially if you are asking them to sow seed into a church project, not tithing, here's what you should do. Instead of appealing to their sympathy, by telling them how great the need is, explain the vision of your ministry. Tell them of the harvest that your church is already producing, whether it is a harvest of souls, or anything else, which would substantiate the validity of your church as "good soil". Then, instead of "asking" them to give, present them an "opportunity" to sow a seed into a project which is "good soil".

Now that we have explained the motivation behind each type of giving, and the rewards as well, hopefully, you will be better informed as to how you may achieve abundance in your life, by taking advantage of God's principles.

After our initial pledge payment of $85.00, our ministry received a check for $850.00. It was much needed and we were shouting "Alleluia"!
[M. C. OF WASHINGTON]

During the Spiritual Warfare weekend in Charlotte, we donated $50, and committed that if somehow, the additional money would come to us, we would be one of the "300". It has been a very lean year for our household, as well as the company I am employed by. I won't get into all the details of the company bonus program, but it is an annual bonus that is paid quarterly. There are also components that are not based on sales. If at the end of the year, you were paid a bonus earlier in the year, and the year end sales numbers are not reached, you owe the money back to the company. There were no sales bonuses due at the end of the year to anyone in our company. I, and several of my counterparts, had been paid a small bonus during the second quarter. I was prepared to have this money deducted from the other rather meager miner bonus due from non-sales related activities. When our Vice President of Sales was reviewing the bonuses with our President, or better yet, how much everyone owed the company, the President stated that "Frank doesn't have to pay back the bonus received in the second quarter". I was the only one he did this for. The VP of sales is still bewildered. But we know why!... This is seed money God intended for your ministry.
[F. J. OF NORTH CAROLINA]

I was in your service when you spoke at our home church. My husband and I have always been givers to God's work, our home church, and other ministers and we thank God for blessing us. My husband owns a well drilling company, which relies on the economy. On Sunday we put our $1,000.00 check in the offering and on Monday my husband got seven new jobs. A local competition called to tell my husband his phone has stopped ringing. All Glory to God.
[L. O. OF FLORIDA]

CHAPTER 9

❧

STOP THINKING
LIKE DIRT

I was in Ivory Coast, Africa, and the pastor who was leading the pastors' conference asked me to receive the offering from the African pastors – an offering to help cover the cost of the auditorium facility where we had held the pastors' conference.

As I looked out across the sea of brown faces, at these men and women who had dedicated their lives to the work of God, something rose in my spirit, and I knew what I had to tell them.

I said, "As you know, I have planted thousands of dollars into Africa, and will continue to do so in the future. God has given me a burden for Africa, and for your country in particular. But every time I come here, I get the feeling that you view me as the rich American who has come here to help the poor Africans."

I continued, "If that is how you are thinking, that means that I am the farmer who is planting the seed, and you are the soil where the seed is planted. That means that when harvest time comes, I will be the one who receives the blessing."

"I certainly don't mind that arrangement, because it means that I will get to enjoy the harvest. But if you are ever going to get a harvest yourself, you must stop viewing yourself as the dirt, and become the farmer who sows the seed. You need to stop thinking like dirt, and start thinking like a farmer."

"How does dirt think? Dirt just sits there, doing nothing, and hoping that someone will come along with some seed. But the farmer says, 'Until I do something, nothing is going to happen.' You need to be the farmer, by sowing a seed so you can enjoy the harvest."

Thank God, many of those pastors caught the vision of what I was saying. It was a paradigm shift for many of them, causing them to view themselves and their ministries in a different light. Later, Pastor Paul, who was leading the conference, came to me and said that it was the largest offering the pastors had ever given at a conference. He thanked me for helping them to "Stop thinking like dirt."

Proverbs 20:4 (NIV) says: **"A sluggard does not plow in season; so at harvest time he looks but finds nothing"**.

How presumptuous must someone be, to look for a harvest, when they know that they haven't planted anything? Every harvest begins with a seed. The sooner we understand that God owes us nothing, the sooner we will accept responsibility for our own lives, and stop thinking like dirt.

When I use the term "Stop thinking like dirt," I am speaking of a welfare mentality. It's an attitude of "entitlement" which causes us to believe that something is owed to us. When my children were growing up, I never gave them an allowance. I realized that many parents do this, giving their children "spending money" each week. But, in my opinion, the child will have a tendency to begin believing that something is owed to them, simply because they have lived another week. In my opinion, that is training them for welfare.

In case you're thinking that I was a cruel father, by not giving my children an allowance, let me explain. I felt that, even at a young age, they needed to learn that any money they receive is a reward for achievement or productivity. I knew that, as they grew into adulthood, and began to go out into the workplace, their bosses would reward them, not for showing up at the office, but for a job well done.

> "YOU NEED TO STOP THINKING LIKE DIRT, AND START THINKING LIKE A FARMER."

Kenneth and Sharah attended a school which

gave out report cards every six weeks. On those report cards, they were graded in seven subjects. For every "A" on their report card, I gave them five dollars. A "B" was one dollar. (This meant that it cost them four dollars if they didn't get an "A.") If they received a "C," they owed me one dollar. For a "D," they owed me five dollars. And if they got one "F" on the report card, it cancelled everything, and they received no money at all, even if the other six subjects received an "A."

If they received "straight "A's" in all seven subjects, they should have received 35 dollars (five dollars for each "A."). But, as an incentive for excellence, if they received all "A's," I gave them a 15 dollar bonus, which meant that they would receive 50 dollars for a perfect report card. 50 dollars every six weeks is not bad, huh? But, they had to earn it. I didn't want them to think like dirt – to have a welfare mentality.

Several years ago, I was speaking at a church, I don't remember where. After the service, a lady walked up to me, obviously upset. With an indignant look, she said, "I think it's terrible that you pay your children to make good grades at school. They should make good grades without being paid to do so."

I replied, "When they get a job, their bosses are going to pay them based on, not only the grades they received in school, but also the quality of work they do on the job. I am teaching them now what they will experience for the rest of their lives."

2 Thessalonians 3:10 (NKJV) says: "**If anyone will not work, neither shall he eat**".

How many times have we cried out to God in desperation, asking him to remedy a situation which was caused by our "lack of planting?" I still remember when Gina and I were in that situation that I referred to in chapter 7. It was the most desperate time we've ever faced in our finances. When I, in a moment of self-pity, asked God to have sympathy on me because of my financial crisis, I expected him to feel sorry for me, and give me a financial miracle out of pity. Instead, as a good father, He simply said, "Plant your way out." He helped me to see that I was not a victim of someone else's actions, but instead, I was a victim of my own lack of planting. Also, to be honest, I was a victim of a lack of good financial management and stewardship on my part. I was "thinking like dirt."

Here I was, teaching my children not to have a welfare mentality, or a sense of entitlement, while I, myself, was guilty of the very same thing.

A few years ago, I was in Pittsburgh, ministering on a telethon for a Christian television network. I was there to raise money for their network, helping them to continue their work of spreading the Gospel through this tremendous broadcast tool. As I was walking through the hotel lobby, I saw a friend, who has had a great influence on my life and ministry, Dr. Mike Murdock. As I greeted him, I learned that he would be ministering on the telethon the following night. So I called my office and asked them to make arrangements to delay my flight, in order for me to stay an extra night and have some time with Mike.

As a side note, I find it amazing, how few people actually take advantage of the opportunities they may have to spend time in the presence of someone whose words and wisdom could change their future. I considered this delay in my travel schedule, and the accompanying financial costs, a very small price to pay, in order to have time with a man of such great wisdom and insight.

As we sat at lunch the following day, I looked at him and said, "Mike, if I don't ever thank you for anything else, I want to thank you for not giving me 43 thousand dollars." He looked at me, confused, and asked me to repeat what I had just said. I then reminded him of something which had happened several years earlier.

In 1997, I felt prompted of the Lord to host a ministry conference at our home church in New Orleans. The conference would be held the last week of January, 1998. This was the first time that Gina and I had ever done anything of this type. Prior to that, I had spoken at many other conferences, hosted by other ministries, but I had never hosted one myself.

In retrospect, I can now see that we really went overboard on the budget for our first conference. We brought in speakers from Australia, New Zealand, and several parts of the United States. The worship leader for the conference was also from New Zealand. With only 200 delegates attending the conference, we had a budget of over 43 thousand dollars.

A few weeks prior to the conference, I felt prompted of the Lord to sow a thousand dollar seed. I told Gina, "I need you to pray with me, because God told me to sow a thousand dollar seed, and I don't know where we are supposed to sow it. All I know is that we need the harvest from a thousand dollar seed."

This is completely different from the way most Christians give offerings. In most cases, they will first identify a ministry for whom they feel sympathy or pity. Then, they determine how sorry they actually feel for that ministry. This results in the determination of the amount of money they will give. In our case, I didn't know where we were going to give. I knew we needed a harvest – a big one. God had told me that it would require a thousand dollar seed. Now, I needed to find the soil in which to plant, which would produce that kind of harvest.

As I was praying, asking God to show me where we should plant that seed, he said, "Sow it into ground that is already producing the kind of harvest you want." I immediately thought of our friend, Mike Murdock. God has blessed and prospered Mike in his ministry, and I knew that this was the kind of soil in which we should plant.

"HOW PRESUMPTUOUS MUST SOMEONE BE, TO LOOK FOR A HARVEST, WHEN THEY KNOW THAT THEY HAVEN'T PLANTED ANYTHING?"

We wrote out the check for a thousand dollars and asked our children to join us as we all laid our hands on the seed, praying to ask for an abundant harvest, before the seed was planted. We then sealed it in an envelope and mailed it to Mike Murdock Ministries.

Again, it may seem crazy and irresponsible for us to give a thousand dollars to another ministry, just weeks prior to a conference which had a budget of 43 thousand dollars. But I knew what God had stirred in my heart, and that this was the right thing to do.

A few days after we mailed that seed, my secretary came to me and said, "Mike Murdock is on the phone for you."

When I answered the phone, he immediately said, "Hey, 'Faith Man,' how are you doing?"

Well, what do you say to that? Obviously, I said, "Hey Mike, I'm doing great!"

He said, "I'm holding your seed in my hand. When my secretary saw your name on the check, she immediately brought it into my office because she knows that we are friends, and that I would want to see it. Tell me, Mark, what are you believing for in your harvest?"

I then proceeded to tell him about our upcoming conference. He already knew about the conference, because when we had asked him to speak, his schedule would not allow him to participate. I told him that our budget was 43 thousand dollars for that week.

He shared some thoughts of wisdom, and some suggestions regarding the conference. As he was speaking to me, it suddenly occurred to me that Mike is very blessed, and that God has prospered him. At that time, although we were not in poverty, we certainly did not have prosperity or financial abundance either. I began thinking that when we sent the check to his ministry, I had no idea that Mike would call me to speak personally about the seed we had planted. But now that he was on the phone, maybe

God would speak to him about sowing 43 thousand dollars into our ministry, so that the conference budget would be met before the conference even started. The more he talked, the more I hoped. After a few minutes, I just knew that he was about to tell me that the money was on the way, and that our budget would be met!

After about ten minutes of conversation, he said, "Mark, God has shown me that your harvest from this thousand dollar seed will come over the next year. One hundred and twenty people will sow a thousand dollar seed into your ministry this year, and you won't have to use this money to pay bills or your staff. You will be able to use all of it for expanding your ministry and to buy new equipment to be used in the ministry. But you need to make a covenant with God and with me, that you will do two things:

(1) That you will faithfully pray every single day for the next year, for each of these one hundred twenty people and their families. You must pray for them for three things: Household Salvation, Healing & Health, and Abundance in Finances, that they will be free from debt. Even though you don't know their names, you must begin praying for them today, and every day for the next year.

(2) Everywhere you speak over the next year, you must tell the congregation that if any of them are sowing a thousand dollar seed into your ministry, that you will be praying for them every day for the next year."

I agreed to make this covenant with God and with him, we prayed together, and said our goodbyes. When I hung up the phone, Gina came to me and asked, "What did he say?"

In a frustrated tone, I said, "NOTHING!"

Gina asked, "What do you mean?"

I said, "He could have written us a check to pay

"WHEN I USE THE TERM "STOP THINKING LIKE DIRT," I AM SPEAKING OF A WELFARE MENTALITY."

for the entire conference if he wanted to. When we gave that seed, I had no idea that he would be calling about it. But now that he called, and he knows about our need, you and I both know that he could write a check for 43 thousand dollars to cover our budget. But he's not sending us anything."

Gina then asked, "You were on the phone with him for quite a while. Didn't he say anything else?"

"Yes," I said. "He said something about a hundred and twenty people giving us a thousand dollars this year, but who knows whether that will happen or not. We are facing this conference in two weeks with a budget of 43 thousand dollars, and he did nothing to help us!" I was frustrated, feeling sorry for myself. I was angry with Mike, because he didn't "come to my rescue." Quite honestly, I was "thinking like dirt." This wasn't Mike's conference. It wasn't his responsibility, and he didn't owe me anything.

Two weeks later, the conference ended with a deficit of approximately 20 thousand dollars. I was still frustrated, feeling self-pity. But throughout the next year, I lived up to the covenant I had made with God and with Mike Murdock. Every single day, I prayed for a hundred and twenty people who would sow a thousand dollar seed into our ministry that year, 1998. And everywhere I spoke, I informed people that if they were one of the one hundred and twenty who were sowing a thousand dollar seed, I would pray for them faithfully every day, for the following year, which I did.

"I AM CONVINCED THAT, OFTENTIMES, IN OUR ATTEMPT TO BE BENEVOLENT TOWARDS THOSE IN CRISIS, WE INTERRUPT WHAT GOD WAS DOING IN THEIR LIFE ON A MUCH HIGHER LEVEL."

On December 30th, 1998, one day before the end of that year, I had lunch with two friends; a friend of mine who is an evangelist from the New Orleans area, Jesse Duplantis, and a businessman from New Orleans who was a mutual friend of both Jesse and myself. As we sat together, enjoying our meal, the businessman said, "I am so glad that I am with the two of you today, because I need to get some more seed in the ground before the end of the year."

Jesse and I were both quite happy to be the ground in which he would sow seed. That day, MJ, the businessman, handed me a check, and became number one hundred and twenty for that year. Here it was, December 30th, the next to the last day of the year, and it had happened exactly like Mike had said that it would. Also, as a side note, none of those one hundred and twenty thousand dollar seeds had to be used to pay bills or to pay staff. It was all used to expand our ministry, to purchase new equipment and to support missionary work outside of our ministry.

The following year, more than 200 people sowed a thousand dollar seed into the ministry. In 2000, at least 300 sowed a thousand dollar seed, which has continued each subsequent year. And I still carry with me a list of the names of each of those people who sow each year. I pray over that list every single day for those same three harvests (Household Salvation, Healing & Health, and Abundance in Finances).

As I sat at lunch with Mike Murdock, in Pittsburgh, relating this entire story to him, a smile broke across his face. It was a look of satisfaction for achievement. The student had learned well from the teacher.

I said, "Mike, I was so upset with you when I hung up the phone in January of 1998, because you didn't offer to send me any money. But now, as I look back, I can see that, if you had given me 43 thousand dollars that day, I would have been satisfied, and I would have stopped looking for anything else. So thank you, for not giving me 43 thousand dollars. Because, if you had, I wouldn't have had the blessing of seeing so many hundreds of people partner with our ministry in this way over the years."

I am convinced that, oftentimes, in our attempt to be benevolent towards those in crisis, we interrupt what God was doing in their life on a much higher level. I'm not saying that you should never help someone in need. But I am saying that sometimes, when you act as the hero, by removing their crisis, and solving their problem, you actually reinforce the paradigm which they have embraced – "thinking like dirt." If God directs you to give alms to someone, or some cause, follow His leading, obey Him, and you will be rewarded accordingly. But don't allow yourself to be led by your emotions, particularly sympathy, in these situations.

I have a really big heart. I love to help people. One of the most difficult things for me is to obey God when he tells me not to intervene in a particular situation, because he is "schooling" someone to help them stop "thinking like dirt." My heart, my emotions, cause me to want to alleviate their pain. But I know that in my own life, pain has been one of the greatest teachers.

I certainly do not believe that pain is God's first choice. In fact, I believe it is His last resort. But when we fail to learn from all the other "professors" He sends our way, His final alternative is to allow you to experience pain – whether it is the pain of financial pressure, emotional loss, or merely desperation. Keep in mind, I do not believe that God ever causes pain. But I know that He can prevent it. And in His wisdom, when He knows that you have ignored all the other teachers He has sent your way, I believe that He will allow pain to pressure you into learning. But this only works as long as someone else does not come along, with good intentions, and a lack of wisdom, to remove the pain, which was the last resort for you to learn the lesson God wanted to teach you.

Again, if God directs you to give alms, you should do it. But remember, when God speaks to us, he does not speak to our emotions. He speaks to our spirit. If you are being led by your emotions, then I can say for certain that you are not being led by God. The story I just told about Mike Murdock was only one example of how God has used difficulty and frustration to help me learn how to be blessed. Admittedly, I believe that he had tried to teach me in much more gentle ways, but when I did not listen, he allowed the intensity to increase until I listened and learned.

True, I am blessed and prosperous today, but that is the result of many such lessons, which have helped me to "stop thinking like dirt," and to start thinking like the farmer.

My husband and I want to thank you for opening up this opportunity to sow into your ministry. We gave our first check in August and we received a $15,000.00 debt release in September, less than 6 weeks later. God is so faithful to His Word. Our finances continue to improve daily, and we are not looking back.
[G. S. OF COLORADO]

We attended your breakfast seminar in Sacramento. You told us to expect a harvest and write you when it happened. Well, it did! We received unexpectedly $ 5,000! Praise God!
[R. G. FROM CALIFORNIA]

I am one of your "300" that sows monthly into your ministry. I wanted to thank you for your teaching on "The 4 Types of Giving". I thoroughly enjoyed these tapes and learned a lot! I was feeling down because my goal this year was to double my income from my job, and I didn't think it was in range. Then I realized that I have already increased my income by over 20% from last year. All this happened while the company I work for went through a terrible reporting fraud and bankruptcy/restructuring. On top of that, the Lord has given me tremendous favor among my employers and colleagues. It seems so easy to focus on what we feel God "owes" us instead of focusing on how we have been wonderfully blessed. Thank you for the attitude adjustment and for your prayers on my behalf.
[K. K. FROM IOWA]

CHAPTER 10

᪣

How To Own
Your Harvest

Hebrews 11:1 (NKJV) says: **"Now faith is the substance of things hoped for, the evidence of things not seen"**.

The IVP Bible Background Commentary states that the original Greek word for "substance" in this passage, appears in Greek business documents with the meaning "title deed."

This verse actually tells us that our faith is the title deed, or "right to take possession of" what we have hoped for. Think about that.

Imagine that you were informed of an inheritance which you had received from a distant relative, who had left you in their will. Perhaps they had died several years ago, and you did not realize that some real estate in Alaska, which contained very productive oil wells, was part of your inheritance.

That would mean that for all those years, you had owned something from which you had not derived any benefit. Now, someone shows you that the title deed was mixed in with some other documents which you had received some time back, but you didn't see it. What if you were in a financial crisis, needing money, and had declared bankruptcy last year, not realizing that there was oil found on this piece of property, which would more than pay all of your debts, and provide you with financial income beyond that?

Can you see how this would affect you, if you learned that you had lost your home, your car, and other possessions, needlessly – all because you didn't realize that you had the title deed to this piece of property which you had never seen?

Someone may say to you, "But how do you know that it really exists? You've never been to Alaska. Do you know that there really is real estate in Alaska which belongs to you?"

You could simply reply, "I haven't seen it, but I know that it exists, and I know that it is mine, because I'm holding the title deed. This proves that I own it, it gives me the right to take possession of it anytime I choose, and it means that I am the rightful recipient of all benefits derived from it."

That's what our faith in God does for us.

I grew up in a pastor's home. From the time I was a young child, my parents taught me to tithe. When I received money for birthdays, or by doing chores around the house, I knew that the first ten percent belonged to God. Because I was taught this from a young age, it has always been easy for me to tithe, and I have never hesitated to do so.

As I have already stated, I also gave some offerings, but for most of my life, I didn't understand the four types of giving or the motivation behind each, so, for the most part, I gave alms, because my giving was usually motivated by sympathy. If a missionary came to the church and showed us photos of starving children in some starving land, I would feel sorry for them, and give an offering. If a guest minister spoke at our church, and I knew that they had a great need in their life, out of compassion for them, I would give in their offering. Today, I understand why I didn't receive substantial increase from that giving. It was all motivated by sympathy, which means that I was giving alms, not seed. And, as I have already stated, the reward for alms is merely a reimbursement of the amount you gave. Therefore, I could never "get ahead" by giving only out of sympathy, because there would never be true increase resulting from that giving.

"THE AMOUNT OF SACRIFICE NOT ONLY AFFECTS THE WAY GOD VIEWS OUR OFFERING, BUT IT ALSO AFFECTS HOW WE WATCH FOR OUR HARVEST."

Several years ago, when Gina and I were going

through our worst financial crisis, I was on a plane, flying from New Orleans to Alabama, to preach. As I sat on the plane, having just taken off from New Orleans, I quietly prayed. I said, "Lord, you see how terrible our financial situation is. Please help us. Please give us a financial breakthrough."

As you can see, I was "thinking like dirt". I was expecting God to feel sorry enough for me, that he would feel obligated to intervene on my behalf. I was praying with a welfare mentality.

He said, "For years you have been tithing. You have submitted your finances to Me. James 4:7 (NRSV) states: **"Submit yourselves therefore to God. Resist the devil, and he will flee from you"**.

God showed me how that, although I had submitted my finances to his authority, I had not been taking full advantage of the benefit derived from that. This verse explains that after we submit an area of our life to God, we can then use the authority to resist Satan's activity from that part of our life.

Because I had been tithing, submitting my finances to God, I had access to authority which I had never used. God said to me, "My word does not say, 'submit yourself to God, and the devil will eventually leave you alone.' It says that after you submit, you must resist the Devil before he leaves."

This was a revelation to me. It was as if a light came on in front of me, and I could see clearly, where I had never seen before. As I was praying, seated on that plane, I quietly said, "Satan, I am submitted to God in my finances. I have authority over you. In Jesus' Name, I bind you, and I command you to take your hands off of my finances. God's Word says that the thief must repay seven times what he stole. You have been stealing from me for years. In Jesus' Name, I command you to loose into my hands everything you have stolen from me financially, and pay me back seven times what you stole."

I arrived in Nashville, to change planes for my trip to Alabama. As I was waiting for the flight, they made an announcement,

"Ladies and Gentlemen, this flight has been overbooked. We need volunteers who will take another flight. If you are willing to do this, we will give you a voucher for a free flight with our airline."

I said, "That's me!" I went to the counter, received my voucher, and they rerouted me through Atlanta, Georgia.

On the flight to Atlanta, I prayed a similar prayer, binding Satan from my finances, and commanding him to loose into my hands, everything he had stolen from me, paying back seven times what he stole.

Believe it or not, when I arrived in Atlanta, waiting for my flight to Alabama, they made an announcement, "Ladies and Gentlemen, this flight has been overbooked. We need volunteers who will take another flight. If you will do so, we will give you a check which you can cash immediately."

I said, "That's me!" I went to the counter, received my check, and they rerouted me again. I went to the payphone and called the pastor who I would be preaching for the following morning. I asked him what time the service started the next day, because I wanted to get as much as I could out of this situation, while I was "on a roll"!

I finally arrived at about 1:30 AM and preached the Sunday morning and evening services. On the Monday morning, I was a little late getting to the airport. As I approached the counter, the man asked me which flight I was on. When I told him, he said, "Oh no! That flight is overbooked. We are taking people off that flight right now."

I said, "Excuse me. Do you need me to take another flight?"

He replied, "Oh, yes sir! That would be so kind of you."

"Hey, Harry, don't worry. This man said that he is willing to take another flight."

I said, "Wait a minute, wait a minute......what'll you give me?"

I got another free flight!

God was using this whole situation that weekend to teach me that I had rights to financial privileges, which had gone unused all of my life. I wasn't using my "title deed". I owned it, but I was not benefiting from it, because I didn't realize it was mine.

What I've been telling you up until now in this chapter is only what I learned about the benefits of tithing. Remember, the tithe and firstfruits are the foundation for all other giving. But the giving which produces the greatest return, by far, is seed.

A couple of years ago, I was preaching at a church in Staten Island, New York, which is a part of New York City. The evening service was about to start. As I walked down the aisle of the church to find a seat, a young man approached me. He said, "Brother Mark, do you remember me?" It always makes me nervous when people ask that. I meet hundreds, possibly thousands of people every year. Remembering their names would be impossible. Recalling their faces is even difficult at times.

Thankfully, I did remember meeting him the previous year. I said, "I believe you told me that you are called to preach." He said, "That's right!" I went on, "And I believe that your wife was expecting a baby when I met you.". He answered, "That's right, too!" (I had gotten it right on two out of two. I wasn't going to try for more.)

He said, we became one of your 300 last year. I said, "well, I didn't remember that, but if you joined the 300, your name was on the list that I've been praying for every day."

He said, "Oh, we know that you've been praying for us. We've felt the results of that! In fact, shortly after my wife gave birth to our first child, in January of this year, she received a phone call about a job offer. She now teaches at a private, Christian school. In fact, that was our harvest. When she got that job, our income

"THERE IS ALWAYS A HARVEST WHEN WE SOW A SEED."

> "IN ORDER TO
> GET WEALTH,
> YOU MUST GO
> AFTER IT – YOU
> MUST PURSUE IT
> – AND YOU MUST
> BE WILLING TO
> PUT FORTH THE
> EFFORT AND THE
> WORK NECESSARY
> TO DESERVE IT."

doubled. We now make 32 thousand dollars a year!"

I stood amazed, in disbelief. Had I heard correctly? Did this mean what I thought it meant? I was almost horrified as I thought of what he had just told me.

I asked, "Do you mean that when you became one of the 300 last year, pledging a thousand dollars to our ministry, you were living in New York City, one of the most expensive places to live in America. Your wife was expecting your first child, and you were making only 16 thousand dollars a year?"

He smiled and nodded, "That's right!"

I thought, "What is wrong with this guy? How irresponsible of him to pledge one sixteenth of his gross salary to our ministry when he was making that little, and they were expecting their first child!" At that moment, I decided that I was going to find a way to get that money back to him, even if I had to give it out of my own pocket.

The service was starting. As I quickly made my way to my seat, the young man cheerfully said, "And we're going to be one of the 300 again this year!"

I thought, "What is wrong with him? Some people never learn!"

As I sat there, God spoke to me, "You are not going to give that money back. He received his harvest. His income doubled."

I said, "But look how little he was making before it doubled!"

Then God reminded me of a verse of scripture which I have used many times when teaching on harvest. But in the light of what this young man had just told me, I now understood that verse in a new way, better than ever before.

Proverbs 10:5 (NIV) says: "**He who gathers crops in summer is a wise son, but he who sleeps during harvest is a disgraceful son**".

God asked me, "Why would someone sleep at harvest time?" You see, my dad grew up on a farm. He has told me on more than one occasion, how everyone conducted themselves at harvest time. When the fields were ripe for harvest, there were no vacations, no days off, and you worked from daylight till dark. Because there was a brief window of opportunity in which you could gather in the harvest before it began to rot on the vine. During harvest, time is of the essence, and everyone helps.

When God asked me why someone would sleep at harvest, He then answered His own question. "The only reason they would sleep at harvest is because they have nothing invested in that field. Daddy paid for it. If we lose the harvest, it's Daddy's loss, not mine."

God went on to say, "Mark, how many harvests have you slept through, because you had so little invested in the field, that you didn't even feel it when you planted the seed?" He explained, "The reason this young man didn't miss his harvest is because it was such a sacrifice to sow this seed. He had so much invested in that field, there was no way he was going to miss his harvest."

Think about it. How do many Christians give? They say, "OK, after we pay all of our bills this month, how much is left over? Now, take that number, divide it by your social security number, take 1/3 of that, and we'll give half of that." By the time you get down to that amount, you don't have any sense of sacrifice, and you didn't exercise any faith to give what you have extra.

When Jesus taught his disciples by using the example of the widow's mite, he helped them to see that God always views what we give, not simply as a dollar amount, but more importantly, by the amount of sacrifice involved. But what God was teaching me through this young man in New York, was that the amount of sacrifice not only affects the way God views the offering, but it also affects how we watch for our harvest.

Genesis 8:22 (NKJV) says: "**While the earth remains, Seedtime and harvest, …Shall not cease**".

This means that every time… every time you sow a seed, there will be a harvest. Every time. I'm emphasizing that on purpose. There is always a harvest when we sow a seed. Do we always receive that harvest? No. Why? Because often, there was so little sacrifice on our part when we planted, so little invested in that field, that we find it easy to sleep right through our harvest, and it rots on the vine before we ever see it.

Keep in mind that when it is harvest time, the harvest does not march itself into your barn. God produces the increase from your seed, but you must go to the field to gather in the harvest. I think that often, Christians expect that after they sow a seed, God will simply have the harvest delivered to their door. In some cases, this may happen, as a means of encouragement for your faith. But make no mistake, on a typical basis, there must be activity on your part to garner in the harvest with which God has blessed you.

Sometimes your harvest will come in the form of an idea or a business opportunity which will produce multiplied returns on the seed you planted. Your work and effort in this regard is required in order for the harvest to come into your hands.

Deuteronomy 8:18 (NKJV) states: "**And you shall remember the Lord your God, for it is He who gives you power to get wealth, that He may establish His covenant which He swore to your fathers, as it is this day**".

This verse tells us two things: first, we are told that God gives us the power to get, not

> "WHENEVER I AM FACED WITH ANYTHING, WHICH CHALLENGES MY FINANCES, I IMMEDIATELY SAY TO MYSELF, THERE IS A HARVEST WITH MY NAME ON IT. I REMIND MYSELF THAT MY FAITH IS THE TITLE DEED, THE RIGHT TO TAKE POSSESSION OF MY HARVEST."

the power to receive. God frowns on laziness, and he admires a willingness to work. Wealth is available to us – not for the receiving, or even for the taking, but for the "getting". In order to get wealth, you must go after it – you must pursue it – and you must be willing to put forth the effort and the work necessary to deserve it.

The second thing we learn from Deuteronomy 8:18 is that God's purpose in giving us the ability to get wealth is not merely for us to spend it all upon ourselves. Rather, His purpose is that we should use that wealth to establish His Kingdom on this earth. If you have a heart for building and establishing God's kingdom – for reaching the lost – for helping the needy – for making a difference in this world, God wants you to have wealth.

We started this chapter by referring to Hebrews 11:1 and to the principle taught in that verse, that our faith is the title deed to what we have hoped for. If you are sowing seed into the Kingdom of God, you need to begin saying to yourself, "There is a harvest with my name on it."

Whenever I am faced with anything that challenges my finances, I immediately say to myself, there is a harvest with my name on it. I remind myself that my faith is the title deed, the right to take possession of my harvest. Tithing alone is not enough. Giving of firstfruits is not enough. Giving of alms is not enough. Sowing of seed is not enough. If you don't know how to claim and take possession of the return on what you give, you will never truly have abundance in your life. I encourage you to not only have a generous heart, but to stand on God's Word, in faith, and claim what is rightfully yours.

Let me close with a verse from the New Testament, 3 John 1:2 (NKJV) **"Beloved, I pray that you may prosper in all things and be in health, just as your soul prospers"**.

All prosperity should be measured in comparison to your spiritual condition. Matthew 16:26 (NKJV) says: **"For what profit is it to** a man if he gains the whole world, and loses his own soul? Or what will a man give in exchange for his soul"?

We should never take financial prosperity out of the proper context, in comparison to our walk with God. If you do not already have a personal relationship with Jesus Christ, may I encourage you to pray this prayer with me. "Dear Jesus, I know that I am a sinner. Your Word says that all have sinned, and come short of the Glory of God. I do not blame anyone else for my sin. I chose, it was my own decision. It was selfish, and I am sorry. I regret it. I believe that you are the only saviour – the only son of God – that you left Heaven, and came to this earth, born as a man. You died on a cross for my sin, and physically rose again to give me victory over satan and sin. I ask you, Jesus, please come into my heart. Wash me clean with your blood. I accept you as my saviour, and I make you the Lord of my life. I surrender all my life to you. Now, satan, I am submitted to God. I can resist you, and you have to leave. So in Jesus' Name, I command you to get out of my life. I don't belong to you. I belong to Jesus. Thank you Jesus for forgiving me of my sin. Amen."

If you prayed that prayer just now, please contact our office, and we will send you some materials to help you in your new walk with Christ. We will also help you to find a church in your local area, where you can be fed spiritually. You can email us at **info@markgorman.com**, or call **504-464-4447**, or write to **Mark Ministries Incorporated, PO Box 11325, New Orleans, Louisiana, 70181.**

We were introduced to a new tape series that totally reshaped our thinking. "God's Plan For Prosperity" helped us to see where we were missing the boat. We will be eternally grateful to you for being God's messenger. Since then we decided to sow into your ministry. We have paid very close attention to the money that we receive, whether it be in the form of a bonus check from our business, a bonus check from my job, or even tax returns. As we watched the money flow in we knew that God was supplying us seed. After we made the decision to go ahead and sow the seed, God has given my husband a new job that is very promising. He is now in a Christian owned company that will give us the income we need to meet our needs and allow us to continue to plant into ministries.
[H. F. FROM ARKANSAS]

I'd like to give you an offering report. When you visited my church, my fiancé (at the time) and myself both independently pledged to be one of your "300". Within one week of sowing these seeds, I was promoted and received an $18,000 dollar raise. God's blessing was truly upon us, but it took an act of faith to receive it.
[J. C. FROM CONNECTICUT]

I had to write and tell you how the Lord is blessing us. The day after we made our faith promise to pledge this year, our transmission started going out in our truck. We did not have the funds to have it fixed. I knew that the Lord would have to provide. Well, last Monday, my boss walked into my office and handed me $300.00 cash. That is the exact amount we had to have up front to get our truck fixed. Then Thursday, he walked in my office and gave me a $1.12 per hour raise. My chin was on the floor. All that I could do was utter, "Thank you" and cry. Also, I have been praying for my family to be reconciled to God. I longed for them to have the strong and close relationship that they once had. Well, my aunt called me the other day. I haven't heard from her in over a year. She just began to speak words straight from God and how the Lord has blessed her and her family. My husband

and I must be one of your "300". I can't wait to see what God will do next!
[D. N. FROM LOUISIANA]

More testimonials:

We attended the Dallas Ministry Breakfast in December and made the $1,000.00 commitment in the event it came our way. At the time we made that commitment, we could not imagine where any extra money would be coming our way. On February 1, I was notified that I would be receiving a bonus at my job. This was totally unexpected. We knew immediately where this money was going. Here is our bonus that covers one half of our commitment. I have no doubt that the remainder of our commitment will come sometime this year. This only proves that when you make the commitment, it will happen.
[T. K. OF TEXAS]

Since we became one of the "300" last month, much has happened in our lives. When we attended the conference, I had been laid off from work. Within 10 days of pledging to be part of the "300", I found a new job that pays better, I like it more, I work with mostly Christians now, and the commute has been reduced from 40 minutes to 5 minutes. Additionally, we had been in the process of refinancing our mortgage. Every time a possible problem came up, it just seemed to melt away. Thank you for your ministry and prayers.
[C. K. FROM NEW YORK]

I'm writing to let you know what God has been up to in my life as a result of your ministry. I was at the Spiritual Warfare Conference in Charlotte. I pledged to sow $1000 into your ministry if in the next 12 months, God provided extra that wasn't expected and went above normal needs. I went to Alabama for Easter to take my unsaved dad and brothers to an Easter production two weeks after the conference.

As we were driving to the play, my husband called and asked me if we were expecting a check. It was our mortgage company. They had mailed an escrow check for $1,036.71! I immediately realized that this was our seed. Praise God! I am so fired up! Thank you so much for your ministry and for your awesome anointed teaching.
[W. R. FROM SOUTH CAROLINA]

I attended one of your Partner Breakfasts and pledged $1,000.00 to your ministry. At that breakfast I gave you my first installment of $100.00. Almost immediately after the breakfast, my husband received a job offer from the largest mortgage company in Minnesota. The income potential is impressive, but the best part of the new job was that he could resign from his previous position at a brokerage company that had horrible ethics. He has now finished an extensive training program and has now received his first "real" check. I am enclosing another $100.00 installment to put towards the $1,000.00 that I pledged.
[I. T. OF MINNESOTA]

Personal Note from Mark

Since the first printing of God's Plan For Prosperity, the number one question asked by readers is for more information regarding firstfruits. Keep in mind that when the Bible was written, basically everyone was a farmer to some degree. Because of this, there was no need for an in depth explanation regarding firstfruits. In today's economy, it is sometimes more complicated to determine exactly how to "compute" firstfruits, and to know the amount which is appropriate. I am hesitant to give too much speculation, if I do not have clear Biblical support for my opinion. Therefore, my first suggestion is that you seek God's direction for you and your particular situation. He will direct you. Let His peace be your guide.

Several people have asked what to do in regard to a one-a-year bonus. My suggestion is that you divide that bonus by the number of pay periods you have in a year. Then, the first "taste" would be essentially the amount of that bonus for one pay period. Then, you should tithe on the remainder of that bonus.

Again, I am hesitant to oppose my opinion on anyone else if I do not have clear scriptural direction in regard to Firstfruits. Therefore, I urge you to seek God's direction for you particular situation.

We have created a page on our website to address additional questions regarding the financial principles in this book. To view this page, go to http://www.markgorman.com/FAQs.htm.

About the Author

Mark Gorman has been a public speaker for more than 30 years. He is a minister, motivational speaker, teacher, and recording artist.

Mark and his wife, Gina, along with their two children, Kenneth and Sharah, reside in New Orleans, Louisiana. Mark speaks extensively throughout the United States, Europe, The United Kingdom, Asia, Mexico, Canada, Australia, and New Zealand.

Mark and Gina also speak as a team. They offer keen insights on overcoming the challenges facing marriages and families today.

Mark's unique gift of humor has endeared him to audiences of all ages around the world. His keen wit puts audiences at ease and allows him to communicate with openness and transparency.

As a Christian, Mark welcomes the opportunity to tell people that any successful business principle in use today can be found in the Bible.

OTHER PRODUCTS BY MARK GORMAN

Audio CD Packs

❧ SPIRITUAL WARFARE

Pulling Down Strongholds

Taking the Promised Land

The 3 Kings – Authority for Warfare

The Three Heavens

The Whole Armor of God

❧ FAITH

God Responds to Faith

The Attitude of Huge

Victory in Trials and Storms

❧ MOTIVATION

Don't Give Up

God's Plan for Prosperity

Winners Never Quit

❧ FAMILY

Building Strong Families

For Every Mother & Father

Marriage 101

Winning Your Family to God

❧ SPIRITUAL GROWTH

Contagious Anointings

Don't Water the Trees

Four Types of Giving

～⦿〜

How to Receive the Holy Spirit

Inside-Out Christians

Knowing God's Will

Marked by the Anointing

The Lord is My Shepherd

The Ultimate Paradigm Shift

⦿ MARKETPLACE MINISTRY

Marketplace Ministry Paradigms

Ministering in the Marketplace

⦿ BUSINESS SUCCESS

You Can Succeed

Becoming a Leader

WIN

DVD's

⦿ BUSINESS SUCCESS

How to Keep Your Dream Alive

Getting a Message to Garcia

⦿ HUMOR

Cajun Humor I

Cajun Humor II

For a complete listing of products, please visit our website:
www.markgorman.com.

SPONSORS

Mike & Cathy Abrahamson

Euclid Antunes

Ana Maria Antunes

Philip Antunes

Cassandra Antunes

Sarah Antunes

John & Chris Armstrong

Terry & Elly Arnold

Kip Baker

Angie Baker

Chuck & Anita Bales

Harry "Chip" & Tina Barber

Ghedeon "Doru" Bere

Nicholas Beswick

Mac Blackwell

Peter & Marjorie Blanco

Lisa Boilore

Christopher & Robin Boucher

Margaret Boudreaux

Diana Brennan

Juergen & Sally Brinner

Mary Helen Bryant

Gordon Bunker

John & Rebekah Byrd

Raymond Bysiewicz

Chris & Diana "Duffy" Clayton

Jeremiah Clements

William Clements

Tamara Collins

Bonnie Conner

Michael Cooney

James Cornelison

Allan & Stephanie Coveyou

Dr. Anne Cox

Curtis & Debi Cradic

Jody, Kim & Devin Craft

David & Kay Crompton

Wendy Crowell

Justin Culver

Philip & Linda Cusimano

Rev. & Mrs. Fred Davis

Pam Davis

John & Diana Delin

Charles & Nikki del Marmol

Charles & Mary Frances Denton

Bernie DeSouza

Luke DeSouza

Joshua DeSouza

James Dillenbeck

Lynn & Doris Dugger

Craig & Debra Duncan

Brandon Fahrmeier

Mr. & Mrs. Donald J. Fetters

Dennis Flanery

Carl Engy Florely

Paul & Kim Fontaine

Jim & Kaye Fry

Philip Furlong

Richard & Militza Garcia

Tom & Tina Gardner

Paul & Maralee Gazelka

Lloyd and Billi Lou George

J Don Grassie

Doug & Paula Golay

Rev. & Mrs. Marvin Gorman

D Jack Haines

Lisa Haines

Davy Hall

Pam Hall

Jack & Yvonne Hampton

Stephen & Deborah Hansard

Dave & Barbara Hardeo

Donald J. Headley

Kalvin & Jeanette Henry

Jon C. Henshaw

Craig & Nancy Herren

Heath and Lindsey Hines

Gregory Howard

Patricia Howard

Don & Bonnie Hoyt

Mr. & Mrs. Andrew Hutchinson, Jr

Stephen and Patricia Jamison

Matthew Jaster

Rev. & Mrs. Jerry Jenkins

Michael & Janet Jenkins

Arol Jeune

Jesse & Cara Jimenez

Larry & Katrice Keenan

Dwayne E. Kerr

Craig Kisner

Hope Kisner

Robyn Kisner

Bob Knobbe

Kiara Kriener

Dick & Anne Laese

Dr. & Mrs. Euton Laing

Katherine Leicester

Aaron Levy

Sue Levy

Ed & Stana Libich

Edmund Liu

Bev Lonchar

Justin Lonchar

Kayla Lonchar

Tim Lonchar

Randy & Maureen Lovell

David & Elizabeth Machado

Lynne Mack

Daniel & Lisa Madsen

Cynthia Mallett

Jerry A. Markham

Bill & Betty Jane Marsh

George Martin

Mark & Jennifer Martin

Bob & Lori Matcheski

Raymond C Matz, Jr.

Warner Morris McAlister

Steve, Melanie, Jocelyn & Tatem McCloy

Daniel McMahon

John & Suzi Mennel and Family

Courtenay Mitchell

Rudy & Catherine Mohammed

The Money Tap

Thomas & Jillian Moody

Ken & Judy Mundy

David & Carol Nelson

Miguel & Alma Otero

Michael Palazzo

Don & Pat Patterson

Brian Partlow

Marty & Renee Pecek

Allan & Debbie Perry

Inez Pervorse

Casey T. Phillips

Deborah Phillips

Joe & Tracy Piercy

Fred & Amy Pope

Cole Alexander Price

David & Stacie Ralston

Mike Redenback

Kristian and C. J. Reinbold

Erin Restemayer

Jamie Restemayer

Jim and Pat Restemayer

Michael & Cindy Restivo

Michael Dylan Restivo

Annabella Claire Restivo

David Riedl

Fred Rogers

W. Curtis & LaNita Roland

Chris Ross

Mike Ross

Carolyn Rowden

Marcelyn "Marcy" Sawyer

Scott Schaefer

Alan, Diana, and Victoria Schmitt

Gary Scollard

Molly Scollard

Arnold & Sharon Sefcik

Arnold & Tiffany Sefcik, Jr.

Henry & Verna Mae Sefcik

Gene & RhondaSeiter

Leonard & Michelle Selby

Steven & Angie Seshun

Edgar & Bonnie Sheaffer

Marilyn Hicks Smith

Clayce Spurlock

Sarah Spurlock

Sheila Squyres

Randall Stalter

Joel & Amy Steele

Dave & Lilli Stevens

David & Chris Stevenson

Marvin & Bernese Swallows

Kerry, Susan, Dylan & Skylar Swan

Judy Taber

Stephen Temple

Fran & Marilyn Tenerovich

Bethlehem Teshome

Amy Teske

Nicholas Teske

Cliff & Karen Thompson

Ellen Tietjen

Bobby & Ceci Torres

Anthony & Veta Tortomasi

Matthew & Rachel Trigger

Donald VanDaele

John VanDaele

Patrick & Tanya Van Otteren

Michel Veilleux

Diane Veilleux

Tommy Veilleux

Melvin & JoAnn Verrett

Casey Vogt

Jim & Nancy Vogt

Jimmy Vogt

Johnny Vogt

John & Kathy Vogt

Michael Walrath

Clay & Kimberly White

Frank & Elaine White

William & Alesia Wilson

Brett & Lisa Wininger

Michael Winkel

Sean & Joyce Wray

James "JT" Young

John Yeo Seow Yong